Worth It

don't understand what most digital com
but I want congratulate CEO Dan Price f
us all with a useful economics lesson

Every company has tools of the trade that equip employees to do their jobs, in the hope that they will do them well. Strategic decisions are made with the vestment.

Worth It

How a Million-Dollar Pay Cut and a $70,000 MINIMUM WAGE Revealed a Better Way of Doing Business

Dan Price

The re
edia and
avity w
nly go
ter his

s on social me-
history. Gravity
stories fro   Workers elsewhere who suddenly got
raises from converted bosses who tossed them out like Scrooge after his
epiphany -- even, in one case at an apparel factory in Vietnam.

"This can never work on a large scale."

"If it's a publicity stunt, it's a costly one," writes the
Times noting that the average annual pay a
workers will se

Gravity Payments, Inc.
5601 22nd Ave. NW
Ste. 200
Seattle, WA 98107
www.gravitypayments.com

ISBN: 978-1-7341572-0-8 (hardcover)
ISBN: 978-1-7341572-1-5 (paperback)

Contents

Worth It

1
The Hike

HAVE YOU EVER HAD a moment in your life when someone or something forced you to rethink the way you saw yourself and the world around you? That's exactly what happened to me in early 2015.

Based on the conventional definition of success, my life at that point was going extremely well. I was thirty years old and a millionaire, having started a credit card processing company with my brother a decade earlier and grown it into a multimillion-dollar business with more than a hundred full-time employees. I felt good about the work we, as a team, were doing and the culture we'd created at the company. We were profitable but had gained a reputation for excellent customer service and transparency (two things our industry sorely lacked). I worked hard, but my executive-level salary allowed me to play hard as well. Plus, I was still young and healthy, with plenty of time left to enjoy the fruits of what I believed was my well-earned success. The possibilities laid out before me seemed limitless.

Then, in late March of that year, I met up with my friend Valerie for a hike in the Cascade Mountains outside of Seattle, where I live. I had met Valerie three years earlier and considered her one of my most cherished friends. She was in her thirties, but her life up to that point had been very different from mine. At fifteen, she got pregnant. At sixteen, she married the father and gave birth to her son. At eighteen, she enlisted in the army and went on to complete two tours in Iraq during her twenties. After serving in the military for eleven years, she left active duty and began her reentry into civilian life. She had been living in the greater Seattle area during her last years in the military and enjoyed it so much that she stayed. But making a life for herself proved complicated. On the day we hiked that trail together, she was working fifty hours or more per week at Banya 5, a Russian-style spa in the heart of Seattle, and managing residential properties on the side in an effort to pay her bills and child support.

As we began our climb, I asked Valerie how things were going. "Not great," she said. "My landlord is about to raise my rent two hundred dollars a month, and I'm not sure how I'm going to afford it." I could hear the pain in her voice as she told me she didn't know which expenses she could cut in order to afford the increase. She had considered selling her car, but that would mean giving up her property-management income, which was not an option. She thought about moving to a cheaper apartment, but that would mean moving even farther away from work than she already was. Despite making more than $40,000 per year, she had no room to sacrifice, and the booming, unforgiving Seattle economy kept depressing the value of her salary. Like an unsolvable Rubik's Cube, every spending cut she made led to a new set of problems.

I'll admit I had long been confused by Valerie's financial struggles. "Plenty of people live on much less than forty thousand dollars a year," I told myself. "If she's having so much trouble, she must be mismanaging her finances. There must be some expenses she can cut."

In fact, several months earlier, I had offered to help Valerie review her budget. I was convinced I would be able to help her develop a better financial plan, but as I examined her expenses, it was clear that every single line item was essential. This was not a woman who was blowing her paycheck frivolously every week. This was a woman who was doing everything in her power to improve her financial situation—living on a budget, working two jobs, and cutting as many corners as she could. Yet she could never get ahead due to forces outside of her control. I asked her if she'd considered transitioning to another industry where she could make more money, but the costs associated with switching jobs—paying for courses or training, taking time off work, etc.—were too high. She was stuck, trapped in a negative feedback loop that kept holding her back financially. She couldn't afford to stay where she was, but she couldn't afford to leave either. After our sit-down, I felt terrible. I didn't know how to help her, and it angered me that she was in this situation. It didn't seem fair.

Given the severity of her circumstances, I had assumed Valerie's was an isolated case and that her financial woes were the result of years of unique hardships that made her situation more complicated than most. But as I racked my brain on that hike, trying to come up with a way to help her, a troubling thought occurred to me: about one-third of the people I employed at my company were earning less than what Valerie was making. If she was struggling, so were the people for whom I was responsible. If her rent was going up, it was likely a lot of my team was facing the same predicament. I was also keenly aware of another, much smaller, group of employees, including me, who were taking home huge amounts of money. I, like most business owners, had been setting pay based on the market value of each employee—what I could get away with paying someone based on their particular job and experience. But were the highest-paid employees really adding that much more value than the lowest-paid ones? Just because the market said a sales rep was worth more than a support rep, did that absolve me of any responsibility to pay the latter a living wage?

Mental dominoes began to fall. I remembered a study I had read, by psychologists Daniel Kahneman and Angus Deaton, which found that a person's well-being continues to increase up until they earn a salary of around $75,000 a year. At that point, the study suggested, people are able to cover their basic needs and a little extra and thus feel financially secure enough that their lives are stable. Beyond that number, any extra dollar has marginally less value because it doesn't significantly improve a person's welfare.[1]

How could I justify paying an employee less than what Valerie was making when those people were willing to cancel a Friday-night date or work through a holiday to help our clients? Every day that I paid them less than they needed to be financially secure—even though I could have afforded to pay them more—I was actively chipping away at the well-being of my team. How was that productive? How could I let this stand? I knew I had to do something. I wasn't sure exactly what it would be, but the change had to be bold. There had to be a new floor, a new minimum wage for our team.

In April 2015, just after that hike with Valerie, I announced my decision to implement a $70,000 minimum annual wage at our company, Gravity Payments. The announcement created a media frenzy I had no way of anticipating, and I suddenly found myself at the center of a larger conversation about whether businesses have a responsibility to pay their workers a living wage. I received praise, criticism, and outright scorn from journalists, pundits, businesspeople, and ordinary folks who were either inspired or horrified by the decision. Profiles were written, letters were sent, and comment sections were filled by observers trying to unpack my motivations. Was I a bold entrepreneur trying to make a statement about income

1. Daniel Kahneman and Angus Deaton, "High Income Improves Evaluation of Life but Not Emotional Well-being," *Proceedings of the National Academy of Sciences* 107, no. 38 (September 2010): 16489–16493, https://doi.org/10.1073/pnas.1011492107.

inequality in America? Was I a militant socialist out to destroy capitalism by redistributing wealth? Was I a philanthropist trying to give back? Or maybe I was just pulling a publicity stunt designed to drum up attention for my small but growing company.

It's true that at the time of the announcement, I was concerned about increasing income inequality in the United States, and that is still something I worry about every day. As of today, a CEO at one of America's largest companies earns 271 times more than the typical worker.[2] And in 2017, 82 percent of all new wealth created worldwide went to the top 1 percent of earners.[3] Study after study reveals that over the last fifty years, the rich have gotten richer while the average American's wages have stagnated and, in some cases, gone down in terms of real-dollar value.

Traditional business wisdom would say that companies don't need to concern themselves with this issue; as long as companies are paying people what the market deems they're worth based on their skills and contributions, they are paying fairly. Although I'd previously questioned this approach, I didn't see the true failure of this system until I heard about Valerie's

---

2. Lawrence Mishel and Jessice Schieder, "CEO pay remains high relative to the pay of typical workers and high-wage earners," Economic Policy Institute, July 20, 2017, https://www.epi.org/files/pdf/130354.pdf.

3. Oxfam, "Richest 1 Percent Captured 82 Percent of Wealth Created Last Year While Poorest Half of the World Got Nothing," press release, January 21, 2018, https://www.oxfamamerica.org/press/richest-1-percent-captured-82-per-cent-of-wealth-created-last-year-while-poorest-half-of-the-world-got-nothing/.

financial struggles. My income was a lot higher than Valerie's, but had I really contributed more to society than she had? Did creating a successful company mean I deserved to have a better life than a young single mom who had served her country for most of her adulthood? I didn't think so.

The decision to increase Gravity's minimum wage also represented something deeper and more fundamental than a desire to prevent my employees from dealing with the challenges Valerie was facing: it represented my commitment to running a company driven by its values instead of the dollars it earns. It represented the moment when I decided to ignore conventional wisdom and do something I felt, deep down, was the right thing to do. It represented my belief that who you are at work reflects who you are in life; true leadership requires you to uphold both your personal and professional values.

It took me years to figure out what kind of leader I wanted to be, and even longer to translate that desire into action. Growing up in Idaho, I had internalized a simple business philosophy based on a rural American worldview: a company exists to help the people it calls clients. Period. I originally started Gravity because I saw a need in the market I could fill. Although I always wanted the company to succeed, I based every decision on whether it benefited my clients, not on how much money I could make.

As Gravity continued to grow, however, I was thrust into corporate America. I felt the pull from financiers, consultants, and others who wanted to plop Gravity on the standard conveyer belt to success by reducing expenses and maximizing revenue, with little regard for how this strategy would affect anything but the bottom line. In some cases, I was able to resist this pull, but other times I gave in.

My drift toward conventional business thinking was especially prominent when it came to employee pay. By essentially letting the market determine salaries, I could get away with paying the lowest amount necessary to retain the people on our team. For years, I didn't consider the negative impact this had on my employees. It never occurred to me that I should be responsible for making sure they could pay their bills, start a family, or save for retirement. As long as I was paying competitively, I thought I was being fair.

My philosophy on pay was further supported by the fact that the vast majority of people at Gravity seemed happy in their jobs. They were smart, creative, and full of energy. I prided myself on having created such a dynamic company that attracted high-performing people. (As I write this, fifteen years after I founded Gravity, we still have people on staff who have been with us since the beginning—including our first-ever full-time salaried employee.) Surely, if I weren't compensating my employees fairly, they would have left by now, right?

Prevailing business wisdom justified my compensation policy. The most efficient businesses were those that produced the greatest amount of revenue while keeping costs as low as possible, so why pay someone one dollar more than what you can get away with? Ever since the 1970s, when economist

Milton Friedman put forth the idea that a company exists to maximize shareholder value, executives have adopted this philosophy as gospel. Walmart became the country's largest retail chain by micromanaging costs, most notably payroll. The company continued to thrive even though many of its frontline employees were living hand-to-mouth. After taking the helm at General Electric in the 1980s, Jack Welch instituted his "rank and yank" strategy of firing the bottom-performing 10 percent of his employees every year—a strategy he used to generate unprecedented growth and profitability. More recently, a handful of Wall Street executives were rewarded with huge bonuses despite having caused the worst economic crisis in the United States since the Great Depression. While some hemmed and hawed at the unfairness of it all, the vast majority of those in charge accepted the status quo and continued doing what they had always done—making money at any cost. This was the direction I was headed—and I hadn't even paused to question it.

I could have continued to pay people the exact amount the market determined they were "worth." I could have continued to collect a seven-figure paycheck until cashing out my shares and selling Gravity to the highest bidder. I could have retired early, bought myself a yacht, and traveled the world, all while patting myself on the back for the jobs I had created and the wealth I had generated for myself and a handful of others. I could have done all that and called myself a "success," and no one would have argued otherwise.

After hiking with Valerie, however, I realized that success, for me, meant something vastly different. Beginning when I was a child, my parents had taught me what it meant to lead a fulfilling and meaningful life. For them, both devout Christians, this meant dedicating your life to God and letting Him guide your actions and decisions. You didn't do things because they were fun or easy or because everyone else was doing them; you did them because they were the Christian things to do and they brought you closer to God. Although I no longer share my parents' religious zeal, I have never given up this drive to find purpose in my life and act in accordance with that purpose. On that hike with Valerie, I realized I had a huge opportunity to close the gap between my beliefs and my actions, even though conventional wisdom would tell me—and did tell me—I was crazy.

It's become something of a cliché in business to say that in order to get ahead you need to take risks, but rarely do we turn this philosophy inward. We make bold investments. We launch a product the world has never seen or start a company when we know that statistically it's likely to fail. In other words, we are willing to take risks—to a certain point. Faced with the decision to risk our reputations, our wealth, or our standing in certain spheres of power, we often balk. When asked to take a stand, question assumptions, or act on our values, we look for ways to justify inaction or we cite others' behavior as an excuse for our own. As a result, we often end up as part of a system and adopt a philosophy we don't believe in.

In order to make progress, each and every one of us, especially those of us in positions of influence, needs to take these types of risks. The idea that "It's not personal; it's business" is no longer valid. Business *is* personal. It is a human invention that along the way has lost its humanity. When we separate our personal values from our professional ones, we give up one of the most powerful tools at our disposal to effect real change. Whether you're an entrepreneur, an individual contributor, or a CEO, every decision you make about how to run your organization or execute your job affects the lives of those around you and therefore can have a profound impact on society.

My decision to pay a base salary of $70,000 a year at Gravity resulted from my lifelong journey to understand my purpose in the world. Thanks to my upbringing, I learned early on what it means to have a strong sense of purpose and values, but it took firsthand experience in the business world to understand how difficult—yet how important—it is to translate these principles into action. As my company became more successful and I became responsible for more people, I realized that my opportunity to make an impact had increased dramatically. Eventually I understood that squandering this opportunity would be just as wasteful as a wealthy person blowing his fortune at the poker table. From that point forward, there was no turning back. I had to act.

I was willing to take this risk even if it meant losing everything. And even though it hasn't been a smooth ride—I almost lost my company, a few employees and clients left, I had a very personal and very public falling out with my brother, and multiple people attacked me online and in the press—overall, the risk paid off. Since the year before the policy took effect, Gravity has tripled its revenue and employees have reported changes to their lifestyles consistent with those proven to increase well-being. Meanwhile, I've received calls from dozens of other entrepreneurs and executives asking for advice on how to institute similar compensation programs at their own companies. Some of them aren't yet in a position to pay a full $70,000 a year, but they're committed to doing what they can for their people.

I wrote this book not as a manual on how to institute a $70k minimum wage at your company but as a defense of doing business your way and thinking for yourself instead of letting others think for you. My best advice for leaders who want to be more effective is to never take advice. Yes, it's important to gather information and facts in order to make responsible decisions, and there is often great value in hearing the opinions and experiences of others. But true leaders need to follow their instincts and do what they think is right, even if it flies in the face of the well-intentioned advice of others.

Plus, not taking advice might actually make you *more* successful. It's easy to find examples of business "truths" that have been proven wrong over the years. Research is already showing that the old ways of doing business—pandering to shareholders, motivating employees through the promise of financial rewards, measuring success through profit—are no longer working (if they ever really did). My guess is if you really stopped to question the status quo, you would come to these conclusions without the assistance of brilliant economists or psychology PhDs. Employees are drawn to leaders who hold values compatible with their own and are willing to bring these values to bear in their businesses. The time is ripe for experimentation.

What follows is the story of my journey as an entrepreneur and CEO. I share the events and experiences that helped shape who I am as a person and a leader and made me realize I had a responsibility to act in line with what I felt was most important. For me, this culminated in a decision to raise salaries, but you may reach a different conclusion, depending on your own values and circumstances. I hope that in reading my story you will come to appreciate the opportunities you have to improve society through the work that you do and will be inspired to reject conventional business thinking in favor of humanity. Whether you're a CEO, a business owner, a board member, a manager, a politician, a volunteer, an activist, an employee, or any other member of society, I hope you will take the time to reflect on your purpose and, most importantly, translate that purpose into action. If you are willing to take risks, make sacrifices, reject greed, injustice, and ego, I promise you will look back and say the words I now say all the time: *worth it.*

2

My First Mentor

MY EARLIEST BUSINESS EDUCATION came from my father, Ron Price. Raised in Michigan, he was ten years old when his parents divorced. Shortly thereafter, he began smoking two packs of cigarettes a day. In high school, he became involved with a local theater company and for the next few years toured the United States and Europe with the group. During that period, he also worked part-time in his dad's tire retreading shop.

His life continued in this fashion until one day, when he was eighteen, a group of his friends dragged him to a coffeehouse that doubled as a halfway house for homeless people, drug addicts, gang members, and vagabonds. The house was run by members of the Jesus Movement, a religious group formed in the '60s as a response to the drug-fueled hippie culture of the time. That night, my dad and his friends stayed up until 2:00 a.m., rubbing elbows and swapping stories with the eclectic clientele. Before they left, one of my dad's friends asked if my dad wanted to accept Jesus as his savior. My dad was not particularly religious at the time, but he didn't want to be rude. He bowed his head and prayed with the group before heading home.

When he woke up the next morning, his whole perspective on life had changed. He didn't feel physically or emotionally different; he just realized that for the first time in his life, he cared about discovering God's will. There was a new clarity to his thoughts, and he understood that his current life trajectory wasn't right for him. He wasn't meant to be an actor; he was meant to dedicate his life to God and find a career that would allow him to support a family and serve others.

The transformation was abrupt and total. He stopped smoking, left the theater company, and began working full-time for his father's business. He gave himself over to his faith and started what would turn out to be a lifelong practice of praying every day. My father believed that if he worked hard and was patient, he could develop a direct, personal relationship with God through prayer. He also believed that with practice, he could hear divine messages that would help guide his life.

In addition to his work for my grandfather, and in an effort to continue his religious education, my father also became a lay minister, doing financial and administrative work at the nearby Shiloh Fellowship, which started as a Saturday-night prayer meeting and grew into a church. The religious devotion practiced by Shiloh's congregation was highly disciplined, so much so that it would later be investigated as a potential cult by local journalists. But what outsiders saw as suspicious was to Shiloh's congregation simply a way to connect with God and support one another.

The woman who would become my mom, Pam, also worked at Shiloh Fellowship. She did administrative work, supporting her brother, who was the senior pastor. The job put her close to my dad, and after several months of working together, he finally drummed up the courage to ask her out. On their first date, my dad told my mom he thought they should get married. My mom's response? "I've been thinking that for three months."

They married five months later.

My dad always felt an obligation to provide for his family. After working at Shiloh for nine years—and fathering the first four of what would eventually be six children—he felt the need to do something different. After months of prayer and fasting, with the church's encouragement and support, he and my mom moved our family to Milwaukee. The goal was to plant a new church, but this never worked out. Instead, his career took a turn after my mom became interested in a green-juice product that was sold through direct sales. While he was initially skeptical about the way the product was sold, he was impressed by how many customers touted the juice's benefits and decided to join my mom in a home-based business.

What my dad lacked in experience or training, he made up for with his supernatural drive. He believed that while you might not be as smart, rich, or qualified as someone else, you could always outwork the competition. He worked long hours building his client list and soon began moving up the ranks of the company. The juice company employed a dubious multilevel marketing strategy, so his job involved both selling products to customers and recruiting customers to sell more products. My dad's work ethic earned him modest success in both areas, but where he really shined was in public speaking. Thanks to his acting background, he was an incredible presenter who could hold your attention on any subject from the Bible to the benefits of organic juice. The company leadership quickly noticed his skills and moved him to their headquarters in Idaho. There, he gave training seminars to new salespeople and continued to climb the corporate ladder. After a decade of service, he became president of the company.

The hard work paid off, giving my parents the opportunity to support our growing family. My brother Jesse, eight years my senior, had come first, followed by Lucas, Nicholas, and then me. The four of us were born in Michigan, and my only sister, Emily, joined the rest of us rug rats during our stint in Milwaukee. A couple of years after we moved to Idaho, our family became complete with the addition of my youngest brother, Alex.

My parents named me Daniel Joseph after two important figures in Christianity. In the Bible, Joseph's brothers hated him and eventually sold him into slavery. Joseph worked his way out of slavery and ultimately ended up as the chief administrator for all of Egypt. In this position, he helped the kingdom survive a great famine and saved the lives of the brothers who had betrayed him. Like Joseph, Daniel suffered his own share of ill fortune. After conspirators tricked King Darius into condemning Daniel to death, Daniel was thrown into the lions' den, where the king assumed he'd be eaten by morning. God, however, deemed Daniel innocent of the crimes of which he was accused and sent an angel to close the lions' jaws. Finding the prisoner unharmed and absolved, Darius released Daniel, who went on to achieve high administrative positions. My dad said God had told him I would be an administrator one day, which is why he picked those two names.

When our family relocated to Idaho, we settled in Nampa, a small, rural town about thirty minutes outside of Boise. Our house was several minutes' walk away from that of our closest neighbor, and we had to drive twenty minutes to reach the nearest gas station. The setting suited my parents just fine, however, as it gave them the space to raise their kids the way they saw fit.

My parents' religious convictions only grew stronger over time, and they were determined to pass this zeal down to their children. My father would wake up around 4:00 a.m. every weekday to pray. An hour later, my mom would wake me and my siblings by flipping on the lights to our bunkrooms. After a short period of preparation, we would begin family Bible study, sitting around a table with our parents, who supervised. We always read one psalm, one proverb, one chapter of a gospel, and one other excerpt from both the Old and New Testaments.

I certainly didn't enjoy waking up hours earlier than most other kids my age, but that predawn Bible study was the only regular quality time I got to spend with my dad. As Dad's responsibilities at work grew, he traveled to Asia several times a year, and even when he was stateside, he often wasn't home.

He'd leave the house at 7:00 a.m. on weekdays and typically not return until 9:00 p.m. or later, when I was already in bed. He tried to make time for us on Sundays after church, but he was usually so exhausted that he'd sleep all day instead.

Although my dad may not have been present in my day-to-day life, he shaped me in other ways. From as far back as I can remember, I admired my dad more than anyone else. I envied his poise, charisma, and willpower. He was the type of person who, if he said he was going to do something, just did it, with no excuses or backtracking. He was also a dedicated, lifelong learner. In addition to his careful study of the Bible, he was an earnest student of Stephen Covey, especially Covey's seminal work, *The 7 Habits of Highly Effective People.* While the book does not explicitly deal with faith or religion, it does have religious undertones and is rooted in certain Judeo-Christian values to which my dad could relate. My dad recommended the book to everyone he met. He knew the majority of the chapters by heart and took every opportunity to teach others about them. Since I wanted to connect with my dad, I read *The 7 Habits* as soon as I was old enough to read. By the time I was eight years old, I could recite all seven of the habits and explain them as articulately as most adults.

But my father didn't simply recite Covey's work; he continually sought ways to put Covey's recommendations into action. The second habit, "Begin with the end in mind," encourages readers to ask themselves, "What is the one goal you would give up everything else to accomplish?" When I was in elementary school, my dad sat us all down in the living room and presided over multiple strategic-planning sessions in which our family determined what we wanted to accomplish in life. The result perfectly encapsulates my parents' view of the world: "Our family mission is to glorify God by loving one another, being good stewards of that which He has entrusted to us, and sharing God's love with others."

My dad was especially fond of Covey's fourth habit, "Think win-win," which advises you to try to figure out a solution or deal that will work for all parties involved, rather than only getting the best deal for yourself. My dad took this concept even further, explaining to us that there was no such thing as a win-lose deal, only win-win and lose-lose deals. If you tried to pull one over on your customers, you might gain something in the short term, but your dishonesty would come back to haunt you, and both sides would eventually suffer. This philosophy was put to the test when the owners of my dad's company wanted to shift focus from their primary juice product to an untested bath oil. My dad believed in the benefits of the company's juice, having witnessed and researched its effects on the people who used it, but he thought it was premature to tout the positive effects of this oil until more research had been done. He didn't think there was a way to put together a win-win deal for both the company and its customers by promoting the bath oil, and his view eventually led to a falling-out between him and the owners that resulted in my dad leaving the company.

My dad spoke so clearly about business. He was deliberate

and logical, linear and self-assured. I loved and emulated everything he did, which pretty much centered on his work and faith. I envied his obsession with work, and I set out to follow in his footsteps. I tried starting my own businesses—from worm farms to landscaping to snowplowing. My most "successful" venture, when I was about eight years old, was selling stationery door-to-door to my neighbors in Nampa through a company that catered to enterprising children. The company paid me a $2 commission on every package sold. I started to get some steady customers, who in retrospect bought more stationery than they ever could have used. It took me a while to understand I wasn't some brilliant salesman; they were just trying to humor an eager neighborhood kid.

Despite my inauspicious beginning in sales, my dad was happy to be my mentor. While other dads took their kids to work and forced them to sit in lobbies or file papers, my dad allowed me to dive into the fray. On several occasions, he had me act as his assistant during sales presentations at the juice company. I listened carefully, and when he called, "Next slide, please!" I leaned forward, clicked the button to advance the slide, and listened in awe as he launched into his next topic. I observed every movement he made and every reaction from his audience. When my dad spoke, people listened. They focused their eyes directly on him. They smiled when he was speaking lightheartedly; they wore concerned, sympathetic expressions when he was being serious. They never looked bored or distracted. Audience members often approached me after the presentations and told me what a positive impact my dad was having on them. He was a masterful presenter and influencer. I left each meeting swelling with pride.

Although my dad was my primary role model, my mom provided the majority of my "standard" education through a loose homeschool curriculum. She homeschooled every one of her kids through elementary school. As my siblings and I got older and began to get involved in more extracurricular activities, she struggled to get us all where we needed to be, which made it even more challenging for her to accomplish everything that needed to get done. My mom didn't always enjoy the work of managing such a large household, but through the lens of her religion, she perceived these tasks as her duty. Like my dad, she saw having a stable, big family as a sign of her devotion to God. She wanted to feel like she was doing her best.

Given how busy she was, it's no wonder my mom wasn't always fully engaged in my school lessons. My parents valued education (my two oldest brothers were valedictorians of their respective high school classes), but by the time I came around, they simply did not have the bandwidth to make sure I was doing my work. While going through my mom's version of elementary school, I developed a system—I would watch TV at the lowest volume at which I could still hear it and listen closely for my mom's footsteps on the floor above. If she started walking toward the entrance to the basement where I was "working," I would quickly turn off the TV, open a book, and pretend to be doing schoolwork. My saving grace was our lack of cable channels. This ensured that I at least watched semieducational shows during my hours of screwing around. Mr. Rogers, Big Bird, and Kate Monday were all professors in my homegrown education.

It wasn't that I didn't care about school or wasn't interested in learning; it was simply never my top priority. Thanks to my parents' teachings and our rigorous Bible study, I believed that God had given me the two greatest things any person could ever want: an omnipotent creator who loved me unconditionally and the promise of everlasting life in heaven. As long as I was a good steward of the Lord, my consciousness and my desires would be preserved for eternity. Nothing was more important than that in my mind, so traditional education always took a back seat to faith.

The fact that I was homeschooled, coupled with the fact that we lived in a rural community, meant my only opportunity to meet kids my age was at church. We attended church on Sundays, Wednesdays, and at least one other day per week. Growing up surrounded by my father's influence and raised on serious conversations about theology and business, I was always more comfortable interacting with adults than I was with kids, whose impulsivity and youthful ideas of fun I didn't understand. Most of my church friends were just as socially inept as I was (many of them were also homeschooled), so our relationships were awkward. We stuttered and mumbled our way through conversations or sometimes just sat in silence. It wasn't your typical childhood playgroup, but, for us, it was enough.

In order to spend more time with my friends and in an effort to increase my commitment to the teachings in the Bible, I signed up to be part of the Junior Bible Quiz (JBQ) team when I was ten years old. The JBQ was an intense competition that consisted of a Bible memorization contest complete with *Jeopardy!*-style buzzers. The moderator would ask a question such as "Who can become God's children?" and contestants would respond with a passage from the Bible: "John 1:11–12. He came to that which was his own, but his own did not receive him. Yet to all who received him, to those who believed in his name, he gave the right to become children of God." I started studying for three hours every day and competed in many local JBQ competitions. I began working my way up the national rankings, and Bible memorization became a large part of my life. I enjoyed the thrill of competition and the fact that all of this work would ultimately help strengthen my relationship with God.

Next to religion, my main interest was business. In the Price household, the line between the two often blurred, creating a quintessentially middle-American philosophy. My parents, especially my father, believed that earthly possessions and money were signs of devotion to God. Proverbs 13:4: "A sluggard's appetite is never filled, but the desires of the diligent are fully satisfied." As long as I put forth the effort, God would take care of me.

Like many Americans, my parents' Christian, pro-business beliefs made them solid supporters of the Republican Party. We listened to Rush Limbaugh every day for three hours from 10:00 a.m. to 1:00 p.m., Mom piping the broadcasts through the house by way of an intercom system to make sure we could all hear what Rush had to say. I can still sing all of his jingles. My personal favorite was set to the Beatles' "All My Loving" and chided Bill Clinton for his fiscal policies: "All your money / I will tax from you / All your money / I need revenue." Limited government, low taxes, and minimal regulation—my whole family nodded along as Rush shared his opinions. I wasn't old enough to vote, but I thought if the Republicans could control all branches of government, the world would be saved forever.

Rush Limbaugh notwithstanding, my early life did not fit neatly into rural American conservative tradition. For example, ours was one of the first households in our area to recycle. Long before large triage centers sorted glass and plastic, and long before trucks picked up bottles and cans curbside, my mother drove everything that wasn't garbage to the industrial recycling center forty-five minutes from our house. And long before celebrities posted filtered shots of their vegan macro bowls on Instagram, the entire Price family followed a vegetarian diet. Years before the organic movement hit mainstream culture, my mother grew much of our food behind the house, pesticide- and herbicide-free. Such lifestyle choices might have seemed incongruous compared with those of other members of our church, but my parents were not, as many Limbaugh listeners proudly asserted themselves to be, "Dittoheads." They learned through independent thought regardless of what their neighbors, a radio host, or an institution said. They meticulously connected their own values to their actions. For them, Christianity was about appreciating what you have, loving each other, taking care of the earth, and especially caring for the poor. My parents never let politics get in the way of those issues. Even when they had little disposable income, they donated money to religious causes that supported the poor and homeless. Whenever politics clashed with religion, religion came out on top with little fanfare.

My parents' example ended up being a catch-22 for them. Of course, they hoped their children would grow up in their image, internalizing their values and continuing to dedicate their lives to God. But their emphasis on thinking for oneself and constantly learning would ultimately lead each of us to develop our own ideas about how to live and what it means to be successful. Today, my views on politics, religion, and business differ greatly from those of my parents, but I still credit them for helping me become who I am.

3
Unlikely Rock Star

IN SEVENTH GRADE, I transitioned into a real school, Nampa Christian, a church school with an evangelical mission. There were about eighty kids in my class, which meant everyone got to know each other quickly. It also meant it was extremely easy to stand out from the crowd.

As the first day of school approached, my anticipation mounted. For the first time, I would be spending my days with other kids my age. Although I had no evidence to support the idea, I expected to do well, both academically and socially. But I was in for a rude awakening. Unfortunately, my ability to recite Bible verses and habit of quoting Stephen Covey weren't effective tools for gaining popularity, even at a Christian school. I didn't know how to dress or how to act, and my attempts to be cool often backfired.

In an attempt to fit in, I saved up to buy one brand-name item of clothing: a Rusty Surfboards T-shirt with a picture of a surfer riding a wave on the back. At first, I wore it every chance I got, but it turned out that wearing the same shirt three-plus days a week, brand name or not, did not make you cool. The other kids made fun of me, so I settled for wearing it twice a week—which no one seemed to notice—and donning my usual hand-me-downs and Goodwill finds the other days. I was always envious of the kids who didn't need to make those trade-offs. One day, I was in the locker room getting ready for gym class when Kyle, one of the coolest guys in our class, walked in wearing a nice brand-name sweater. He strutted over to his locker and pulled the sweater over his head. Underneath was a brand-name T-shirt! He had so many cool T-shirts that he didn't even have to show them off. Christian or not, middle schoolers care about the most superficial things, and I was no exception.

My fortunes took a turn for the better when one of my classmates, Nate, a member of the "in crowd," invited all the boys in our grade—about thirty people total—over to his house for a party. When I found out Sean, another classmate of mine, was going to be there, I knew I had to go. Sean was one of the most popular and worldly kids at my school; he'd even kissed a girl, which basically made him a hero among the boys in my class. The opportunity to be seen hanging out with guys as cool as Sean and Nate was too good to pass up.

On the day of the party, I and about twenty other kids showed up at Nate's house, where we basically just hung out for a while. At one point, Sean, who was a drummer, noticed a drum set that Nate's parents had set up for Nate's younger brother. Nate came from a family of talented musicians—his dad played guitar, and Nate was a skilled guitarist and singer himself. He and Sean started jamming while the rest of us watched in awe. After cranking out a few Nirvana covers, the two twelve-year-old rock gods announced they were going to start a band. "We need a bass player," Sean said. "If you own a bass and know how to play it, you can be in our band."

Excited whispers rippled through the crowd. It was clear this was a real opportunity. Playing in a band with two of the coolest guys at school? Sensing this was my ticket to success and undeterred by my lack of skill, I decided to buy a bass, even though I'd never played one in my life. Several other people were interested, but I had one advantage: thanks to the odd jobs I'd worked and small businesses I had started, I had been saving my own money for years. While the other students were saving up or convincing their parents to buy them a bass guitar, I walked over to Dorsey Music and bought one of their cheapest models. After that, I reported for duty.

Sean and Nate weren't initially thrilled with their new band member. Not only did I not know the instrument, my presence in the band certainly wasn't going to heighten our popularity. They took me in nonetheless. We loved the music of Nirvana, Green Day, the Offspring, and similar mainstream bands, but for the sake of parental approval, we primarily played Christian punk rock. After trying out a couple different band names, we settled on Straightforword, which highlighted our connection to the word of God and our commitment to being "real" and original.

We started off playing at classmates' birthday parties, but

things really picked up when our school asked us to headline its annual fundraiser concert. Two hundred people showed up, including five members of our favorite local rock band, F4X (a shorthand version of their full name, Fools for Christ). After the show, the members of F4X told us they loved our sound and asked if we would open for them on their upcoming regional tour. The band members were in their early twenties, making them ten years our senior. We couldn't say yes fast enough.

Despite the standard parental misgivings about sending their kid out on the road with older strangers, my mom and dad decided to let me play with the band. Most of the venues were within a few hours of Nampa, but none of us were old enough to drive, so we hitched rides with other bands or had Sean's mom drive us.

After several shows on tour with F4X and other groups, we boasted thirteen original songs and a few covers. Unfortunately, drinking-age restrictions limited the number of places where we could perform, and there weren't many venues that allowed underage kids to attend shows. If we wanted to keep our momentum going, we'd have to get creative.

Luckily, a friend of mine had an older brother, Jared, who worked as a barista at a local coffee shop called Moxie Java. He introduced us to Heather, the owner, and we convinced her to let us set up a stage. Since the venue was small, we played an acoustic set. During our normal shows, we rarely played covers, but on this occasion, we decided to make an exception. We played "Free Fallin'" by Tom Petty, "My Hero" and "Everlong" by the Foo Fighters, and "Eye of the Tiger" by Survivor. The performance was a huge success: fifty people attended, and we netted about $250 on ticket sales. We decided to do a few more shows at Moxie Java, and the coffee-shop sessions soon became a regular gig. For the first couple shows, Heather let us keep all the proceeds from our ticket sales. She was happy making money selling nonalcoholic drinks to our fans, and I was proud of the fact that I had negotiated a deal à la Stephen Covey's fourth habit: "Think win-win."

Things continued like this for several months until one day when I came to Heather's shop to book our next gig. She told me she was going to have to dock our ticket sales if our fans purchased with a credit card. Confused, I asked her why.

"Because the credit card processing company charges me this huge three percent fee on all transactions."

"That doesn't make sense," I said. "All they do is take money from one place and put it in another. Why would they charge so much?" She told me to wait at the counter while she retrieved something from the back. She returned with a stapled packet.

"This is my credit card processing statement from last month," she said, opening the packet to a random page. I noticed that most of the numbers had minus signs in front of them, denoting a debit from Heather's bank account. I couldn't believe what I saw. It wasn't Heather who was stealing three percent of our revenue, it was this big company whose name I had never heard.

"Can I keep this?" I asked.

"Sure," she said.

I took the statement home and showed it to my dad, who by this point had left his job at the juice company and was consulting in the credit card industry. I asked him to help me figure out how to reduce Heather's credit card processing fees so the band wouldn't lose so much on ticket sales.

For consumers, using a credit card is easy. You pay for goods or services with a swipe, and at the end of the month, you get a bill. For businesses, however, the system is expensive and opaque. Every time a customer swipes a card, the business is charged a fee, generally ranging from 2 to 4 percent, depending on the size of the transaction, the type of card used, and the rate charged by the credit card processor. The processor then moves the money from the bank that issued your credit card to the bank account of the business where you made the purchase. If the processor's systems ever break down or something abnormal takes place, business owners can find themselves stuck in a wasteland of phone trees and responsibility-shirking customer-support personnel as they try to track down their daily deposits. To add insult to injury, at the end of the month, the processor debits the business's account for a huge sum of money, equal to the sum of all the transaction fees for that month. For most small businesses, it's the fourth-biggest expense on their ledger behind payroll, cost of goods, and rent.

With the help of my dad, I did some research and returned to Heather's shop several days later. Together we called the credit card processing company, and after a few minutes on the phone, we were able to negotiate a lower rate and save her a few hundred dollars per month. It was that easy. We hung up the phone, looked at each other, and smiled. At the time, I had no idea the impact this short interaction would have on my life. All I knew was that I felt great. Not only had I helped Straightforword put a little extra cash in our pockets, I'd helped an entrepreneur I admired make her business a little leaner.

Heather wasn't the only business owner I came to know while I was in the band. The Record Exchange, a famous record store in Boise, took a risk on us and began stocking our CDs even before we had much of a following. There was also a group of high-traffic local restaurants and shops whose owners allowed us to post flyers advertising our upcoming shows. Without their willingness to advertise for us, we wouldn't have had the attendance necessary to support ourselves. Karleen, the owner of the local Hogi Yogi franchise, was one of our biggest supporters. While standing in line for frozen yogurt, there was a good chance you were going to see a Straightforword poster. Through each of these interactions, I began to develop a deep love and appreciation for the independent business community. I idolized every owner I met. They were the self-determined businesspeople my dad had taught me to revere. They exemplified grit and determination. They were risk takers. They worked incredibly hard but still made time to support our band. I felt as if I were mingling among celebrities.

Throughout eighth and ninth grade, as the band's notoriety increased, we started playing bigger and bigger shows. Like a real rock star, I dyed my hair red (people told me I looked like Raggedy Andy) and painted my fingernails in a multicolored rainbow. I jumped and thrust about on stage. I went from having no friends to being a social hero. Our songs started playing on a small network of Christian-rock radio stations that blasted our music across the country. The station was royalty free, so we didn't earn a dime from airplay, but it did help us get more exposure than we'd ever imagined.

We stopped opening for other bands and became the headliners. We signed on to play the Extreme Tour, a regional tour that used music and other events to connect with at-risk youth. The tour gave us the opportunity to travel throughout the western United States for months at a time. Because we only played tour shows every second or third day, we found ourselves with a lot of free time, so we called other local venues to try to book more gigs in town. Our hustling allowed us to perform at some well-known venues, including the famed Whisky a Go Go in Hollywood, but the pinnacle of my music career was the final show of our biggest tour. We were back in Boise, and five thousand people attended a show called "Light in the Night." I have a picture I took over my shoulder with the crowd screaming our name and singing the words to a song I had written. I was on top of the world.

Things were going well, but my situation was tenuous. My social standing was based solely on my position in the band,

and my relationship with my bandmates was fragile. We were teenagers, hardly mature enough to handle everyday interpersonal differences, let alone those that come from being on the road and running what was essentially a business together. Resentments inevitably grew, especially when it came to our various responsibilities within the band. For instance, I knew we needed money to fund our activities. Touring was generally a break-even endeavor, and since we didn't earn any money from radio play, our only profit came from selling CDs, T-shirts, and other merchandise. After a show, I would throw my gear in Nate's parents' twenty-year-old Suburban before running back into the venue to mingle with our fans and sell merchandise. Sean and Nate were meticulous in the way they packed their instruments, and although they hated the thought of being salesmen, they still got mad at me for shirking roadie responsibilities. After one big show, having just sold more than $100 worth of merch, I returned to the car, where Nate and Sean had just finished loading our stuff.

"It took us half an hour to load the van," Nate complained. "We had to pull your amp and all your stuff back out so that we could fit our gear in there."

"We need to sell stuff," I replied, getting defensive. "We're not going to be able to continue this if we can't pay for it."

"So, you get to go hang out with all of our fans, while we do all the grunt work?" Sean said. "I don't think so."

We fought about our assumed roles for months. Every once in a while, we would come to a delicate compromise wherein I would help load some of their gear before heading back inside to meet our fans, but this never sat well with my bandmates. We started fighting more frequently, and I began to wonder what would happen if the band broke up. Would I revert back to being the awkward, unpopular kid I'd been when I was twelve? Would I lose the improbable music career I had come to love? I was the worst musician in a successful band that was responsible for all of my social clout. I had built up a fragile facade of popularity that could come crashing down at any minute.

After my sophomore year of high school, my nightmare scenario unfolded. Despite the success of our big concert in Boise, the results of our latest tour had been lackluster overall. There were too many empty venues, and tensions in the band began to build. Sean was the most talented musician in the group and was always being pitched by other bands that could offer more money and prestige. He stuck with us for a while, but after the tour ended, Nate started taking side gigs with other bands and began showing up late for rehearsals. Frustrated with Nate's lack of commitment, Sean finally pulled the plug. Straightforword officially broke up.

Rock stardom had placed social success in my lap, but without the band, I didn't have what it took to make it on my own. Teenage angst kicked in—hard. I walked around school with a hood over my head and refused to speak to anyone for weeks. I brooded over my rock career and began to imagine how I could continue it. Eventually I came to the conclusion that I was going to be a professional musician. I would be the front man for a new, better band. Sean and Nate had been holding me back from my true creative potential, I told myself.

The delusions of future grandeur continued until I confided in my friend Jared, the same guy who had introduced me to Heather at Moxie Java. Jared was three years older than me and in many ways interacted with me like an older brother. He was always giving me advice, whether I asked for it or not.

He listened to my fantasy for several minutes before saying, "Dan, you're an okay bass player, but the two guys you were playing with are really exceptional. You have no chance of making it as a professional musician. You've peaked."

I didn't want to believe him. I immediately went on the defensive. "What?" I countered. "How can you say that?" I offered excuses and pointed out small flaws in his argument. He listened calmly, with all the confidence of someone who knows he's right.

"Sean and Nate were the real talent in the band. You don't have the skills they have, but you have something else. You were most responsible for the band's success."

Now I was confused. "Why do you say that?"

"It was your work as band manager that allowed the band to sell CDs and book gigs. Sean and Nate didn't like the business side and weren't very good at it." I thought back to our arguments about loading gear versus hawking merchandise. Jared's words began to make some sense. I suddenly realized that for me Straightforword had not just been a chance at fame or the first step toward a career in music; it was an opportunity to actually use all of the business know-how I had been learning from my dad. I was following in his footsteps, building a business and spreading the word of God.

For several weeks, I thought about what Jared had said. Eventually, I realized that the reason I enjoyed being band manager was not just because it was an opportunity to flex my underdeveloped business muscles. It was also the love and connections I had built with the people who had supported us along the way. These were coffee shop owners, nightclub owners, bar owners, store owners—anyone who had a stage, a record section, or a blank wall where we could hang posters. Most of these business owners were in the Boise area, so I decided to reach out and see if there was any way I could help them. I started with Heather.

4
Teenage Entrepreneur

MY DAD WORE A SUIT to church and to work, which meant he wore a suit most of the time. So, in an effort to look professional, I took a page out of his book. For my first meeting with Heather, I got rid of the nail polish and hair dye and donned the only professional clothes I had—an oversized suit with huge shoulder pads and a thick red tie.

When I walked in the door of Moxie Java, I could tell Heather was trying not to laugh at my ill-fitting getup. I must have looked ridiculous, but I kept my cool. I asked if I could help her negotiate her credit card processing fees and set up gift-card and loyalty programs. Despite our previous success in this arena, she looked at me as if I were crazy and turned me down immediately. Looking back, I'm sure she just didn't take me seriously because of my age. I stood and left, not disappointed but resolved. I knew I could help her business. I just needed to convince her.

Over the next few weeks, I persisted. Heather clearly felt bad about turning me down, so she started avoiding my calls. I gave up using the phone and went back to the shop to talk to her in person. After I'd cornered her multiple times, she eventually gave in and let me help her reduce her credit card processing fees. I was seventeen years old and had my first client. I did as much as I could for free, because it was fun to learn and I felt like I was making a difference. I helped her set up gift-card and electronic loyalty programs. I helped her wire phone cables throughout the shop and made sure the internet worked. My rock-star dreams gradually faded with every minute I spent at Moxie Java.

Heather was happy with my work and began introducing me to other business owners. Through word-of-mouth referrals during my junior year of high school, I began to build up a base of clients in the area. I helped them negotiate lower credit card processing fees and improve the functionality of their payment terminals. I helped them set up gift-card programs and run phone cables. I helped out at Hogi Yogi; the Toy Store, in Sun Valley; Bogus Basin, our local ski resort; and many more businesses. In turn, these owners referred me to more and more local shops, restaurants, and bars. Soon I had a small independent practice operating as the IT and credit card processing procurement guy for these businesses.

Once I had exhausted the network of clients I had built organically, I decided to try my hand at cold calling. When I approached a local landscaping-supply shop outside of Nampa, the owner chased me out of the store, yelling threats in my wake. The industry's poor reputation had preceded me, and this guy didn't want anything to do with me. And he wasn't the only person. I received a lot of rejections. These business owners dealt with multiple vendors pitching them for their business every day. Whenever some new guy came along to make another hard sell, they put their guard up, and I rarely got the chance to explain how I was different.

I was getting down on the idea of cold calling when finally I met Neil, the owner of Greenhurst Nursery. I was seventeen years old when I walked into his business unannounced and uninvited. I asked if I could help him reduce his credit card processing fees and improve his customer-service experience. For the first time, I didn't receive an outright rejection.

"Yeah, I'd be open to seeing what you could do for me," Neil said after I made my pitch. "I just have one question, though."

"Sure, what is it?" I replied.

"How old are you?" There was a pause. I stared at him. I didn't know what to say. I wondered if I should say I was older than I actually was to make myself look credible. Or maybe I should just give a really low number, so he would know I was kidding but wouldn't know my actual age.

"Twelve," I said with a smile.

"Well, my guess is you're in your twenties, but you look like you're twelve. Come back tomorrow."

I turned and walked away, working to conceal my elation. I was shocked that someone had agreed to another meeting. I came back to the nursery several times, and a few days later, Neil agreed to work with me. I watched him intently as he signed the contract. In that moment, I realized I could make a career out of doing exactly this. This owner had no previous relationship with me but was signing up to have a high school kid help him with his business. I rocketed out of my post-band-breakup funk, and in a matter of months, I went from being convinced that I was going to be a professional musician to being convinced that I was going to help independent businesses for the rest of my life. I dove headlong into my work.

I soon realized that these business owners had many technology issues I could tackle, but the place where I could have the biggest impact was in credit card processing. Every month, massive, faceless corporations plucked several hundred cups' worth of coffee revenue from Heather and her peers. Without a dedicated chief financial officer (CFO) or finance person, these entrepreneurs had no way to defend themselves against sharply increasing fees couched as industry taxes or hidden on their statements altogether. Reducing this cost, even incrementally, made a big difference—sometimes it was the difference between staying afloat and going under. I resolved to focus my efforts there.

The actual negotiation process was pretty unsophisticated. I would call up a bunch of processing companies, ask them the lowest rate they could offer my client, and then get them to bid against each other for that client's business. It would have been simple if the processing companies operated in good faith, but they would inevitably add a bunch of hidden fees to the rate they quoted me, forcing me to pick up the phone once again. I didn't have any special skills—and at the time I knew relatively little about how the industry worked—but I had plenty of time to argue, which is what made me so valuable to my clients. In exchange for my efforts, my clients would pay me a commission—usually somewhere between ten and thirty percent of their savings—though I never asked for a specific rate. I was just happy to be working with them.

Negotiating these fees became a full-time job, supplanting school as my main focus over the course of my junior year. Eventually, though, business owners started calling me, saying, "Dan, you know that rate you negotiated for me on my credit card processing? Well, it stayed there for a few months and then went right back up." Bait-and-switch tactics are rampant in this industry. I started to fantasize about having more control over the transaction processing system so I could manage the fees and keep my clients from being overcharged. Initially, the thought of building the infrastructure necessary to run payments was far too daunting, but the calls kept coming.

The work quickly grew to the point where I had to take time off school to keep up. Fortunately, I was able to make this work through some creative scheduling. After Straightforword broke up, I had joined the school choir and gotten serious about singing. I also continued to work on my bass skills and had arranged to take bass and voice lessons off campus. I used my lessons as an excuse to leave school during the day but padded the time commitment involved in order to have more time for work. I tried to organize my school schedule around my work meetings, but, if necessary, I just skipped class.

I continued wearing a suit and tie to my meetings, and since many of these meetings took place in the afternoon, I often didn't have enough time to change after class. As you can imagine, my attire on those days was wildly out of place for high school. On one occasion, I secured two periods of absence in the morning to negotiate a deal for a local business. The negotiation was successful, but it went longer than expected. I missed third period and received detention. As I stayed late after school, I thought back to the deal I had worked out and smiled. It was worth it.

Sometimes I worked all night and only slept for an hour or two. Rarely did I sleep more than six hours. I would do my homework during class so I didn't have to do it later. I tried to pay attention to the teacher as well, but, believe it or not, some teachers frowned on this type of multitasking. In those classes, I just slept. Some teachers at Nampa Christian paid more attention than others, so many didn't even notice my eyes were shut. I remember one particular theology class. I had the material down, and most of the class was doing test prep. I told Nate, who was sitting next to me, to wake me up when the class was over. Of course, he forgot. The teacher finished the class and turned the room over to another teacher and a dozen underclassmen. They sat there and watched me sleep for several minutes before one of the kids shook me awake. I looked up at this foreign scene, a red imprint of the desk on my face. I didn't wait to determine what had happened. I grabbed my books and ran out of the room, late for my next class. Sleep deprivation was the price I paid for tackling school and business simultaneously, but it was all worth it. I loved the thrill of business, I loved my clients, and oddly, the scarcity of time eventually forced me to manage my schedule better at school, to the point that my grades actually started to improve.

On the job, I was spending much of my time attempting to subdue my clients' ever-rebounding credit card processing fees, but that didn't keep me from having to make the big decision every seventeen-year-old encounters: what to do after high school. Although the pull to focus full-time on my business was strong, I was committed to playing my part in our family's drive for generational progress. Since my mom and dad had not attended college, they felt their job as parents would not be complete unless all of their kids earned diplomas.

Each of my older brothers had attended a prestigious private college, but by the time my turn came, my parents didn't have enough savings left to afford such an exclusive education. Luckily, since I was making my own money, I could afford some of the tuition myself, and when Seattle Pacific University offered me a partial vocal scholarship if I majored in music, I took it.

I decided to continue serving my clients in Idaho remotely while I attended school. Fortunately, not a single one of my two hundred or so clients decided to leave when I told them I was moving away. Content that I could maintain my academic and occupational balancing act, I packed up and moved west, leaving behind my homogenous rural existence in favor of the big city.

Seattle was a change for me. Diversity, in every sense of the word, abounded. Since Seattle Pacific is a Christian university, many of my classmates shared conservative Christian beliefs and backgrounds similar to mine. Outside of the school, however, there existed a collage of viewpoints, ethnicities, and preferences in the city. Despite the shift in environment and increased opportunities for entertainment and socializing, my lifestyle remained largely unchanged. I spent much of my time servicing my client base, spurning the typical fun-filled college experiences. I maintained my religious discipline and went to church every Sunday. While many of my freshman peers exploited their newfound freedom at parties and other social events, I stayed the course.

Transitioning to college in a new state while running a business full-time was equal parts challenging and exciting. But I was also taking on a new responsibility in my personal life.

My sophomore year of high school, I'd met and become extremely close to a girl in my class named Kristie. She and I first got to know each other as study partners, but the more time we spent together, the deeper our connection grew. During our junior year, it became clear that our feelings for one another were more than platonic, and Kristie gave me an ultimatum. Because our faith—not to mention our parents—forbade us from having any sort of romantic or physical relationship before marriage, Kristie told me I needed to get her parents' permission to continue to be a part of her life.

I agreed and asked her parents out for coffee. They got straight to the point. "Is your intention to marry our daughter?" Kristie's dad asked. "Because if not, you can't keep seeing her."

I didn't know how to respond. Kristie and I weren't even technically boyfriend and girlfriend—we'd never even kissed! I was seventeen years old, and still in high school. How was I supposed to know if I wanted to spend the rest of my life with this person?

I assumed my inability to commit meant that Kristie and I would have to end things, but later, when I confessed my dilemma to my dad, he encouraged me to think about it differently. "If you were born in any other time or even most other places in the world today, at seventeen, in this situation, you'd probably get married," he said. "You should think about it."

I took my dad's advice. I still wasn't convinced I was making the right decision, but I trusted him, and I didn't want to abandon my relationship with Kristie. I told Kristie's parents I intended to marry their daughter, and Kristie and I headed into adulthood as a couple.

After graduation, I moved to Seattle, and Kristie moved to Illinois to attend Wheaton College. The distance was hard, but we spoke often, and I was so busy with school and work that most days flew by in a blur. Toward the end of my first semester, I considered transferring to a school in Illinois so Kristie and I could be closer. I loved Seattle, but I figured Chicago would be just as good a place to grow my business, and the institution named on my degree had never mattered much to me anyway. I mentioned the idea to Kristie. "Eh, it's no big deal," she said. "I don't really like it here anyway. I'll transfer over there."

The following semester, Kristie moved out to Seattle and into a dorm a few blocks away from mine. One night during our sophomore year, I invited Kristie out to dinner and officially proposed. We married in August 2005.

While I was trying to figure out how to conduct myself in a committed adult relationship, I was also trying to figure out how to grow my business. No matter how much success I saw in my consulting business, I was consumed by the thought of doing something more. During my freshman year, I researched potential vendors, possible clients in Seattle, and the mechanics of starting a credit card processor. I determined the functions and technology I wanted to bring in-house and the ones I wanted to outsource. The business model began to solidify. I had the plan, but I still hesitated to execute it. I didn't know if I could pull it off.

I got the support I needed from my brother Lucas. Six years older than me, Lucas had graduated from college a few years earlier and had since been working as an office manager at a credit card processing company in California. Disillusioned with the company's lack of follow-through and inability to keep commitments to clients and employees, Lucas had quit and moved to Seattle. By the time I started my freshman year, he was trying to figure out which direction to take his career. He considered becoming a schoolteacher, but given the family background in credit card processing, he also saw opportunities there.

One afternoon, he invited me out to lunch at Blue C Sushi, in the bohemian Seattle neighborhood of Fremont. As we ate, he suggested we start a credit card processing company together. "Obviously, we've both been working on our own ideas about what kind of business we could start," he said. "Since we're brothers, we could coordinate and support each other as two separate entities. But I think we should join forces and do this together."

I listened intently to his pitch and remember feeling proud that my older brother wanted to go into business with me. It was just the nudge I needed. Our goals were different, but we both saw synergy in them. Lucas wanted financial freedom, an eventual exit, and an early retirement. He saw entrepreneurship as an opportunity to get these things. I wanted a venue where I could have enough control to make credit card processing fair for independent businesses. We thought that if the company turned out to be successful, both of us would get what we wanted.

We took a walk after lunch, and finally I agreed. We eventually settled on the name "Gravity" because it was easy to say on the phone and we thought it sounded big and independent. Without Lucas's early involvement, I don't know whether I would have had the courage to get started when I did.

Together we plunged into our new endeavor. The first thing we needed to do was secure a primary technology vendor so we could run the network for our clients' credit card transactions. About six months after our decision to start the business, Lucas and I flew to New York to negotiate a deal with one of these vendors.

After stepping off the plane, we tried to find a place to stay. Most of the hotel rooms near our meetings in College Point, Queens, were full, and the only room available cost $300 a night. We were on a tight budget, but since we were young and just starting out, we felt it was important to keep up the appearance that we were legitimate businessmen and therefore didn't consider booking a seedy joint farther away from the meeting. I decided the best option was to book the $300 room and try to get the people we were meeting to pay for it, but this idea made Lucas uncomfortable. Despite misgivings, he half-heartedly agreed to make the pitch.

Lucas is extremely detail oriented, which means he is willing to do the thorough research few others are interested in or capable of tackling. He can spend multiple days studying a single topic to ensure he understands it from every angle. Before the meeting, he had done just that, to the point that he could carry on a discussion about even the most arcane aspects of the credit card processing industry. I was completely incapable of that type of concentration at the time and much more inclined to act as soon as I knew the basics, so having Lucas as a partner helped. Going into that meeting, he was as prepared as it was possible to be.

Partially because we were desperate, and partially because we lacked the professional expertise to ask tactfully, we danced our way around the subject of the hotel-room bill during our meeting. We tried to float the idea several times, but the message kept flying over everyone's heads. Meanwhile Lucas, having done all his research, was meandering from point to point, going through every paragraph of the contract at hand. He understood the technical side, the industry regulations, and even the legal implications of the potential partnership, but his seeming lack of focus on simply getting the deal done frustrated me. Not only was he disorganized, he was also failing to get our room comp'd. I was livid. I tried to interject and turn the conversation back to the point of the meeting, but I was unable to rein in the wandering discussion.

We needed that contract. Without it, we wouldn't be able to operate, and the terms of the contract would determine the price of every transaction Gravity would process. After several hours of discussions, Lucas and I were finally able to get the deal. We left New York with a signed contract but $300 poorer.

A few days later, when we were back in Seattle, the vice president of the vendor called us. "I want to follow up on our meeting the other day," he said. "I'm so impressed with you guys. I am impressed with your energy and with your industry knowledge. You have nothing. You have no assets; you have no history. But there were two things we really respected about you at our meeting. Number one: how diligent you are, how thoroughly you researched everything. You asked amazing questions, and your understanding of the industry is incredibly sophisticated." I was shocked that my brother's circuitous negotiating had been one of our biggest selling points. The VP continued, "And number two: it was so classy of you not to ask us to pick up your hotel bill."

We had the initial contract and had earned the respect of our primary vendor. Gravity lurched forward into existence. The deal immediately gave us good standing in the industry, even though we didn't deserve it. We didn't have any money, but Lucas's deep understanding of how the industry worked bought us the credibility we had no other way of getting at the time.

Between student loans, credit cards, and my savings from the Idaho consulting business, I was able to put tens of thousands of dollars into Gravity to get it moving. No longer completely at the mercy of the larger credit card companies, we finally had a platform with enough autonomy to control the fees our clients paid. I wasn't just the middleman anymore, which meant I was finally in a position to help make credit card processing fair for independent business owners. Just before I spent my last dollar, we managed to get nearly every one of my two hundred existing clients operating on the new platform. The show of support from these first clients was incredible. The fact that they took a leap of faith and switched over to Gravity ensured our financial independence. We were beholden to no one from the beginning. I never could have built the company as it is today without this solidarity.

Our initial fortune, however, did not automatically lead to meteoric growth. Gravity's development was fueled by eighteen-hour pavement-pounding days. At first, I took on the responsibility of soliciting new clients, and Lucas ran the operational side of the business, handling things like accounting and customer service in the days before we could hire people to fulfill these functions. We teetered on the edge of profitability while investing every free dollar back into the company.

Initially, we hired friends and family to help out on a part-time basis, but by my second year of college, we were able to hire our first employees. We started hiring in an unsophisticated way: every time we would hit $2,000 per month in profit, I would hire somebody at $24,000 a year with no benefits, putting our profit back at zero. The first full-time, salaried employee I ever hired was David Meissner, who replied to our job posting on Craigslist. Technically, he was hired to help develop our sales process, but in those early days, we all wore many hats. I know he didn't take the job for the salary, the benefits, or the swanky office. He told me many years later that he took it because he wanted an opportunity to influence and contribute in a meaningful way to the success of a new venture. His salary was less than half the median household income in Seattle at the time, but he never complained and, true to his intent, became integral to our early development. David still works at Gravity, making a solid six-figure income. I wish I could have done better for him earlier. I wish I could have given him things like health care and a 401(k). He definitely deserved them, but we simply could not afford it at the time.

5
Building Gravity

BUILDING A BUSINESS WHILE attending school came with a unique set of challenges. On one occasion, I was trying to close a deal with University Volkswagen/Audi, a major car dealership, over the phone in my dorm room. Ernie, the CFO on the other end of the phone, didn't know how old I was and certainly didn't know that I was negotiating from a dorm room. My roommate didn't care who I was talking to and cranked up the volume on his violent, "shoot-'em-up" video game. I made a mad dash for the closet, wrapped all my hanging clothes around my head to muffle the noise, and continued the conversation huddled in the corner of the closet with the door shut. I closed the deal.

Of course, college itself demanded my attention as well. To fulfill a requirement for my music scholarship, I had to take four days off work during the spring semester of my sophomore year to go on a choir tour in California. I entrusted the business to Lucas while I was gone. By this time, I had taken over all customer-facing activities while Lucas was in charge of behind-the-scenes operations. Before founding Gravity, we had been extremely close, and Lucas had taken an interest in me that was unique compared to how he regarded other members of our family. But since we'd gone into business together, our relationship had become increasingly strained. We argued about strategy, fund-raising, and which business partnerships to pursue. In general, Lucas was looking for fast growth, which required capital, while I wanted to maintain our independence, which required forgoing outside investment. These two forces were increasingly at odds.

As soon as I left for California, things at the company started to go downhill. Clients with whom I had a direct relationship started contacting me to let me know that some of their customer service requests had gone unanswered. I called our customer service manager and asked what was happening. "I guess they just slipped through the cracks," the manager said. His nonchalance was unacceptable to me. I was livid.

"We can't have issues 'slipping through the cracks.' We need to be doing everything and sacrificing everything we can for our clients," I told him. "We need to do better. We need to have higher standards. When I get back, we are going to have some serious discussions about how to prevent stuff like this in the future." I hung up and called Lucas. I told him about the problem and the manager's blasé response.

"Let him learn from these mistakes," Lucas said. "We should accept this level of inconvenience for our clients so the manager can learn. He'll get better when he experiences these things."

"I disagree. Our team can learn, but not at the expense of

our clients." The conversation shifted. "Look, I'm counting on you. I'll be back in two days, but I really need you to step up and take care of this while I'm gone."

Later, I was on a bus with some of my fellow choir members but still fuming about the situation back in Seattle. "I can't believe I'm gone for just four days and my brother can't seem to handle it," I lamented to my seat partner. "How can I trust him after this?" The woman I was talking to clearly didn't care about my struggles, but I couldn't stop myself. I continued to gripe about Lucas for several minutes.

It wasn't until later when I received an email from Lucas announcing he was quitting the company that I learned he had overheard my entire rant. I had accidentally dialed his number while I was talking, and he was understandably upset by what he'd heard. Hearing this kind of talk from his little brother and business partner was the final straw. "You can have the whole company," he wrote in the email. "I'm done."

I was terrified at the state the company would be in when I returned. I let a few hours pass and then sent Lucas an email to see if he was serious about quitting. "I know that you can make the company thrive without me," he replied. "I just don't think that I accomplish much that a good executive assistant couldn't accomplish. In fact, I kind of feel like an executive assistant, and that's just no fun for me." Eventually, we came to an agreement wherein he stopped coming to the office but stayed on the payroll. Unfortunately, this episode was not the last of our disagreements over the way the company should be run. At this point, however, the physical space between us created by the restructuring improved our relationship.

I n those early days, we grew Gravity client by client, working to convince individual businesses to join our growing community. We didn't experience any single moments of transformational growth until late 2006. Several days before Christmas of that year, Seattle was getting ready to shut down for the holiday, and I was preparing to fly to Idaho to be with my family, when David Meissner, Gravity's aforementioned first full-time, salaried employee, went to lunch at a nearby Taco Time restaurant. Taco Time Northwest is a chain of seventy-five Mexican fast-food restaurants in the northwestern United States, unaffiliated with the national brand. They are a family business and have been well run for multiple generations. When David ordered and pulled out his wallet to pay, the cashier informed him that he would have to pay a fee of $0.35 for using his debit card. Annoyed, David grabbed a comment card so he could express his irritation. He drove back to the Gravity office, pulled out the comment card, and realized Taco Time was based in Renton, twenty minutes from our office in downtown Seattle.

Instead of sending in the card, he called the number listed on it and offered to help reduce their credit card processing fees. As it turned out, Taco Time was going through a crisis with their credit card processor. For technical reasons and because of certain industry policies, their processing infrastructure was set to go down in a matter of days. They had called up many of the big processors to try to solve the problem with a new vendor, but none would commit to being able to rectify the issue in the time necessary. Desperate, they agreed to meet with me.

I walked into the Taco Time boardroom three days before Christmas. The business has several different corporate entities, and many of the owners were sitting around the table. They stared at me, a twenty-two-year-old kid in a suit dropped into their midst. One of the executives began to describe their situation: the processing equipment was set to shut down in a few days, and they had no replacement. It was clear they needed a custom solution built and deployed to all of their locations before the shutdown occurred. The problem was so dire none of the other processors could fix it. I knew I should probably follow suit and tell the owners that I couldn't either. We had twelve people—total—on our team, and only two of them were dedicated to installing the processing technology. If our larger competitors didn't think they could take it on, what made me think we could?

I looked around at the faces of the owners and counted the days until Christmas. "I wonder if any of these owners have plans for the holiday," I thought. I started to think about how much time with their families they were going to miss trying to figure out this mess. Like me, they probably had plane tickets booked and vacations scheduled. I wondered how much business they would lose if their credit card terminals were down for several weeks, as would be the case if no one intervened. I felt bad for these owners, some of whom depended on the success of only one or two restaurant locations. Their livelihoods and those of their employees would be severely hurt if they couldn't find a solution. I wanted to tell them it was impossible. Even if I could come up with a solution, my team members were scheduled to be on their own vacations. I imagined having to ask everyone to stick around at the office rather than take much-needed and well-deserved time off. Even if everyone remained at work, we didn't have the manpower necessary to do half the job. We would have to do the equivalent of ten months of work in a week.

But I was also aware that if I turned down Taco Time, there was nobody else to do the job. Our competitors had all passed. We were their only option. As I looked at the grim faces around the table, I felt the same sense of love and respect I had felt for Heather at Moxie Java back in Idaho. Overwhelmed, I realized I couldn't say no. I was going to at least try to find a way to help these people.

I had two problems: First, I had to develop a technical solution to Taco Time's processing problem. Second, I had to install that solution in seventy-five restaurants throughout the Puget Sound region in less than a week, between two major holidays.

I decided to tackle one problem at a time. I thought that if I could devise a solution, then I could start gathering the resources to implement that solution. "All right," I said after everyone had finished explaining their situation, "I'm going to stay up all night if necessary and write up a plan. I don't know if I'll be able to come up with one, but I am going to try. If I can come up with a solution for you, we're going to have limited time to fix this. I'm going to come back tomorrow with my plan, and at that time, I will need a decision from you on whether or not we're moving forward. It's okay if you don't want to give me an answer at that time, but that will mean we can't help." They agreed.

As promised, I stayed up most of the night with our team writing up a plan to keep Taco Time online. There were both technical and regulatory hurdles to overcome. We needed to use new equipment that had only recently been developed and was still untested. At the time, credit card terminals ran on dial-up connections. The first high-speed terminals were just being developed, but because those terminals supposedly took a quarter of the time to download the software needed, they were the only solution that would allow us to get the job done in time. Also, Taco Time didn't have a pricing structure that would allow them to absorb the credit card fees into their menu prices. As a result, we needed to find a way for them to continue to charge customers extra for using their credit cards, a practice that was not allowed by Visa and Mastercard at the time because it discouraged credit card use. Before the sun came up, we had a list of all the equipment we would need and how the plan would work. We also came up with a plan to convert the extra surcharge for credit card use into a discount for using cash, which, surprisingly, was allowed. It produced the same financial result but complied with the regulations.

We had one of the new high-speed beta terminals shipped to our office overnight and planned to do a live demonstration of the equipment at that day's meeting with the Taco Time owners. We tested our solution at the Gravity office an hour before the scheduled meeting. It didn't work. I stared at Dave Dreyer, our technical lead. He didn't look at me but unplugged and replugged a few cords. It still didn't work. He rebooted it. Nothing. The equipment wasn't on the market yet, so there were no manuals or online discussion boards for us to reference. There was no time left for troubleshooting. I made eye contact with Dave. He knew he had to get it to work.

I hopped in the car. While I drove, Dave stayed at the office and called the manufacturer. I tried to drive and troubleshoot, but with no internet connectivity and my eyes on the road, my attempts were futile. I was fifteen minutes from showing Taco Time a $400 paperweight.

I arrived at the Taco Time headquarters, walked into the reception area, and greeted the executives. As they collected the owners and congregated in the boardroom, I called Dave. I was both panicked and angry. "Is it working?" I asked without saying hello.

"I think I have it working," Dave said. "You'll need to download a new file. Can you find an internet connection?"

"Yes."

"Okay. Download this file." Dave gave me the instructions.

I asked the receptionist if I could borrow one of their internet jacks for a few minutes. While on the phone with Dave, I downloaded the new software and prayed it would work. I heard the owners talking amongst themselves in the other room. I felt the pressure of forcing them to wait for me. I watched as the file downloaded to the terminal, the slowly increasing percentage on the screen seeming to taunt me. After three painful minutes, the download was complete. I swiped my credit card and held my breath. It worked. I suppressed a desire to celebrate, unplugged the terminal, and walked into the boardroom.

My flight for Idaho was scheduled to leave in three hours. If Taco Time turned me down, I would get to go enjoy the holiday with my family, relax, and forget about work for a few days. If they accepted, Gravity's revenue would grow by 10 percent overnight, but my vacation would be cut short.

I walked the owners carefully through our solution. When it came time to give the demo, I plugged in the terminal, swiped a card, and clenched my jaw. "It's taking too long," I thought as the transaction processed. Dots appeared on the screen. I could feel the eyes of all the owners on me. I didn't look up. I stared at the terminal. Just when I thought we were going to see an error message, "Transaction Approved" appeared. I used all my willpower to suppress a smile. I peered up with an expression that said, "Of course it worked."

Despite the success of the demonstration, I couldn't quite gauge what the owners were thinking. When I had finished speaking, I gave them a few minutes to ask questions. After asking several, they all looked at each other and agreed to move forward. I experienced ten seconds of elation after receiving that definitive yes, but even before I stood up, my mind turned to the impending task, and the excitement disappeared. The owners cut me a series of checks totaling approximately $60,000 in order to buy all the equipment needed for my plan. It was the largest payment Gravity had ever received. I walked out the door and got to work.

We had never had a client nearly this big or a task this massive before, but these owners had given me money, and I had given them a promise. I called the team on the car ride back to the office and let them know about Taco Time's decision and the work we had in front of us. We now had to install equipment in seventy-five restaurants from Oregon to the Canadian border in just a few days. Personal plans were canceled. Celebrations were abandoned. We stopped all normal operations. Employees brought in family members, spouses, and friends to help; overnight, we doubled our staff to a ragtag group of twenty-five. Our credit card processing militia set to work on an assembly line, putting together the equipment, installing the software, and driving out to every single one of the restaurants. I assigned myself to be part of the deployment team and spent the next five days on my knees dodging stray pinto beans. At every location where I installed the machinery, I ran a short training session with the employees and then drove to the next restaurant.

When Taco Time's old credit card processor got wind of the forthcoming switch to Gravity, they became far less cooperative, refusing to give us any extra time to make the transition before they shut everything down. We raced against the clock. Several of the terminals went out the door with incorrect files on them. When the testing failed, we had to speed the equipment back to the office for reprogramming. We lost valuable hours.

As the deadline closed in, we rushed to install in the last of the locations many miles from the Gravity office. When the final terminal tested successfully before the shutdown, I felt a deep sense of relief. As a company, this event had a big impact on us. It solidified our belief that we could punch above our weight and serve bigger clients. From a practical standpoint, it gave us far more financial resources to build the company going forward. I was amazed at the dedication of our team. I was proud. I bought a few bottles of cheap champagne and invited everyone to the office for a celebration.

In that moment, I thought back to how David Meissner had cultivated the opportunity with Taco Time in the first place. It would have been easy for him to just fill out the complaint form, pawn the problem off on Taco Time, and make himself feel better about the $0.35 slight. Instead he exhibited an initiative that helped not only Taco Time but Gravity, too. It was a win-win scenario—the type of deal my dad had taught me to make. I was proud of all the sacrifices we had made to do this job. I was proud we had canceled vacations. I was proud we had forfeited our plans; instead we would help our clients.

Later, I would realize the harm this philosophy was inflicting on my team, being asked to surrender precious personal time in order to help a company that was not paying them anything close to the salaries they deserved, though if anyone resented me asking them to make this sacrifice, they never showed it. At the time, however, I thought I was doing a good job for the people at Gravity simply because I was resisting the temptation to make other profit-motivated decisions that would negatively impact them. The tumultuous retention of a childhood acquaintance of mine, Matt Sakauye, was a good example of this.

I first met Matt when I was in high school and building my consulting business. He was a few years older and was working full-time in the credit card processing industry for the same company in California where Lucas had worked. I went down to visit Lucas and was introduced to Matt, whose calm presence and composure made an impression on me.

Knowing Matt was still in the credit card processing industry, I called him a few years after Lucas and I founded Gravity. I pulled his number from the actual physical phone book—this was 2007—and set up a meeting in Hawaii, where he had since moved. After I arrived, we swapped stories about the industry, and I told Matt a little about Gravity. Eventually I broached the idea of his joining our team.

"I'll think about it," he said. "Let me come to Seattle and meet everyone."

I agreed, and a few weeks later, after serious internal deliberation, Matt decided to risk his livelihood, take a 40 percent pay cut, and come work for Gravity. For Matt, the risk was worth it because he was looking to be part of a company that was more focused on helping people than making money. He told me he wanted to be able to trust the people he was working with and be in a position to make decisions for the right reasons. He wanted to build Gravity Payments in Hawaii from the ground up in this way. And he did. It wasn't long before he was making an impact. Thanks to Matt's hard work in his first decade with us, we became the largest credit card processor in Hawaii.

In October 2009, Matt's wife, Jessica, gave birth to their second daughter, Reese, four months prematurely. Doctors questioned whether they could justify trying to save her. Reese was taken directly to the NICU, where she underwent several emergency surgeries. The doctors reached a point where there was nothing more they could do; they were sure she would die. Matt and Jessica had never been able to hold Reese. They convinced the doctors to let them hold her at least once before the end.

The doctors took Reese off life support and handed her to Matt. He and Jessica held her for several minutes. During that time, Reese showed signs of immediate improvement. The doctors were baffled, but the improvements were significant enough to put her back on life support and try to save her. The surgeries and treatments continued.

Reese was in the NICU for six months. Taking care of their other daughter, Chloe, while simultaneously handling all of

Reese's medical challenges added up to more than full-time jobs for both Matt and Jessica. There was no way Matt could work, so for nearly a year, he just didn't. We never thought about trying to withhold pay from him. It wasn't a policy, it just seemed like the obvious thing to do. No one ever felt the need to decide.

While Matt was taking care of Reese, everyone at Gravity covered for him. I had recently graduated from college and turned my full attention to work. I spent a lot of time flying to Hawaii to help his team. Hawaii is not a bad place to go, but I already had one stressful job. Two of the four sales reps in Hawaii began to struggle in Matt's absence. They were having difficulty setting sales appointments and were not making their numbers. We had high hopes for them, so I invested extra hours in mentoring and training. I flew there multiple times every quarter, often sandwiching the trips between other work jaunts. I stayed at the cheapest Waikiki hostels and spent my days pounding the pavement with our reps. By putting in extra work, we were able to see Matt through to the end of his time with Reese in the hospital. The two reps eventually started setting more appointments, and their sales numbers improved. As of this writing, they are both still with Gravity. Reese survived and shed the medical problems that plagued her in her first year of life. Matt picked up right where he had left off, eventually growing Gravity Hawaii to fifteen employees and making it our second-biggest market after Washington State.

Although college had presented some challenges, it afforded unique opportunities as well. To augment my real-life business education and get some easy credits, I took a class on entrepreneurship. The professor told me I could just write a business plan for Gravity, turn it in, and earn an A, since the plan was already working to some degree. I did just that, and after the semester ended, my professor encouraged me to enter the University of Washington Business Plan Competition. I didn't have much extra time, but when he told me he could give me more credits—and thus more time for Gravity—if I entered, I decided to compete.

I entered the competition against sixty-three other teams in the Northwest. Some teams represented companies that were still in the idea stage and hadn't earned any revenue yet, while others represented established companies like Gravity. I made it through my bracket and into the final five. Each of the finalists did one last pitch in front of the judges, who were mostly local venture capitalists and angel investors. I spoke about Gravity's commitment to helping independent merchants and about how being a mission-driven organization gave us a competitive advantage. I pointed to our high-double-digit growth rates and laid out plans for how we could continue that growth.

I ended up coming in second place and taking home a check for $15,000—an entire year's worth of tuition after scholarships. More important than the prize money, though, was the fact that the competition gave me some recognition in the Seattle business community. Up until then, I hadn't known the difference between things like "venture capital" and "preferred stock," and the emphasis my competitors had placed on these things was eye-opening. The fact that I hadn't mentioned any outside financing during my pitch drew the attention of one local businessman. He cornered me after the competition and asked if I would meet with a friend of his, Matt McIlwain, a managing partner at the Seattle venture firm Madrona Venture Group. I agreed to take the meeting.

The night before the meeting, I stayed up late researching different terms typically associated with venture investment. One of the concepts I encountered was "preferred stock," a type of ownership that early-stage companies often issue to outside investors. Preferred stock allows investors to own a small part of the company while maintaining significant control over strategic decisions in exchange for giving an entrepreneur money to fund his or her business. Holders of preferred stock often have the power to increase prices, lay people off, cut benefits, or sell the company, even though they aren't involved with the day-to-day operations of the business. When I discovered the fine print associated with preferred stock, I was concerned about whether Matt and I would always be aligned in our objectives if I ended up working with him. It seemed to me there was a strong chance we might end up with wildly diverging goals and I'd have to cede control of the company I'd worked so hard to build.

I also learned that venture capitalists have to go out and raise the money necessary to invest in companies like Gravity, which means they're beholden to their own investors and need to show a return in five to ten years. This means VCs have to structure their investments in a way that allows them to be sold within that time frame. Obviously, you can only sell something if you have someone to buy it, so someone has to buy out the venture capitalists, forcing a new set of investors on the company. Thus, one small initial investment can chain-react into a lifetime of outside influence.

The next morning, I drove to Madrona Venture Group's office, which was located in a tall, shiny glass high-rise in downtown Seattle. Here I was, just a kid, sitting in the office of one of the premier venture firms in Seattle with one of its top investors, who had put millions of dollars to work in the local start-up economy. We shook hands, sat down, and started discussing the future of Gravity Payments.

Matt was interested in investing in Gravity, and the numbers he threw out were extremely attractive: $3 million for 30 percent of the company in preferred stock. This was a huge sum of money for us at the time. We had almost nothing in the bank, and a seven-figure financial boost would have propelled us into a new stage of growth. I told him I would be willing to take the money, but only if he agreed to receive common stock, preventing Madrona from having the power to make decisions that would jeopardize Gravity's mission of helping independent businesses. Matt let me know that was not something they generally did but said he would see if he could make it work.

I came back a few days later to continue the conversation. Matt led me to the boardroom to meet with all the firm's managing directors. There I was introduced to Tom Alberg, Madrona's founder and one of the earliest investors in Amazon; Paul Goodrich, a lawyer and one of Madrona's managing directors; and Greg Gottesman, who would go on to found the tech start-up incubator Pioneer Square Labs. After a brief introduction, the subject of common stock came up. The directors all said there was no way they would make an investment without the protection of preferred stock. The conversation ended right there. I just couldn't get past the fact that at some point the investors would have different ideas about Gravity's direction than I did. I wanted to focus on having the largest possible positive impact on the independent-business community. I knew that if I took this money, I would most likely have to put my investors' concerns over my own sometime in the future. I was not prepared to do that, so I thanked Matt and the other directors and left the office.

Without the distraction of having to satisfy outside investors, I was able to keep my full attention on the business, though it was not easy looking on while risk-tolerant peers and competitors took outside money and grew right past Gravity. Some were able to walk the line between returns and mission, but others were not. Two of my best friends ended up selling their companies for close to $100 million each. Due to the structure of their companies and the lack of independence, selling became a far more attractive option than staying on. At the core, they loved their businesses and they loved what they were doing. They loved their purpose more than they loved the money, but once the cycle of capital compromises begins, getting out—not to mention the major financial windfall associated with doing so—becomes increasingly difficult to resist. After their exits, I asked each of them if they were happy with the outcome. "Yes," they said, touting the financial gains. I then asked them if, after selling, they thought their former companies were likely to live up to the purposes they had set for them. I received two resounding nos. They added that the dreams they'd had for their companies were on life support, if not already dead.

To this day, Gravity has never accepted outside investment, and Lucas and I have been the only shareholders in the company's existence. Many people have asked me, "How can you compete with these big businesses that have all this investment money?" To that I say, "How can *they* compete?" We can actually focus on what we're in business to do and make decisions that serve our customers instead of our shareholders. By opting out of the financing rat race early in Gravity's life, I unknowingly created a competitive advantage for us that would endure. For example, just a few years after my meeting with Madrona, as part of the Dodd-Frank financial reform legislation Congress passed in 2010, card companies were forced to limit the fees they charged for processing debit cards. While many processors pocketed those savings in an effort to please investors and pad their bottom lines, Gravity passed the savings onto our merchants, which made it easier to attract new business.

At the time, though, I second-guessed myself daily. I thought about the business model I had learned from my dad: I was putting my clients first, but was I doing it at the expense of Gravity's success? Were we passing up a shortcut that would allow us to serve our customers better in the future? In hindsight, the answer is clearly no. These venture-backed companies grew quickly, while we had to kick and scratch the entire way. When growth came for Gravity, it wasn't in leaps but in lurches, fueled by the simple principle of working hard to help people. When we needed money, our only option was to help more clients, as they are our only funding source. As with most things in life, there were benefits and there were downsides, but I valued the independence this strategy afforded even if it came at the expense of short-term growth.

With my decision to forgo outside funding, the company seemed to be finally hitting its stride. We may not have been as flush as we would have liked, but we were staying true to our business model of helping independent businesses. We had fought the temptation of outside investment, solidified our independence, and kept our core team intact. I was building the business I had dreamed of since I was a kid—a business run by a team that worked hard to help people. Gravity was becoming the professional manifestation of the life my parents had taught me to live. But even as I began to feel like I had figured it all out, I started to doubt the philosophical foundation on which Gravity rested.

6
Breaking Away

DURING MY SOPHOMORE YEAR of college, I had shelled out the majority of my salary from Gravity—about $2,000 to $3,000 a month—to pay for tuition. My music scholarship offset some costs, but school was still a financial burden. My parents were unable to help, which I didn't mind. I was proud of the fact that I was putting myself through college without their assistance. I thought my parents were proud of me, too, until one day when my dad came to Seattle on business. We sat down to dinner, and he got straight to the point.

"Dan, now that you are becoming an adult, I don't think it's appropriate for your parents to be paying your tuition."

I stared back at him, speechless. My dad had just assumed he was helping with my tuition because he had done so for my older siblings. The words hit me like a punch in the gut. Here was the person whose acknowledgment and respect I had always wanted more than anyone else's, and he didn't even know he wasn't paying for my education. How could someone whom I admired for his business prowess lose track of his own finances? Didn't he realize that I wasn't forwarding any of my tuition bills to him?

I told my dad I'd always paid for my own tuition, but he didn't seem to hear me and continued to talk about the importance of independence. I was confused and upset, but I tried to write off the incident as a fluke. His mistake didn't diminish or negate anything he had taught me growing up. Still, the conversation stuck with me.

In 2008, after I graduated from college, my dad flew to Seattle on business again. He asked me out to coffee and said he had something important to discuss. He had left the credit card consulting gig several years prior and had been out on his own as a business consultant ever since. I asked him how business was going.

"Okay," he said. "But I'm in a little bit of a tight spot right now."

"What's up?" I asked.

"I need twenty-five-thousand dollars or I'm not going to make payroll."

I was shocked. I couldn't believe he was in this position, and I couldn't believe he had come to me for help. I'd always seen him as successful, but in that moment, I started to view my dad differently. His faults and shortcomings, previously obscured by my all-consuming admiration, became clear. Of course I had always known, conceptually at least, that no one is perfect, but somehow I had never considered my dad was anything but. His worldview was so positive. He always saw the best in people and had surrounded himself with like-minded individuals who showered him with praise. Their words had made me so proud, but now I realized how my dad's attitude was failing him. He was too optimistic and too trusting and was inclined to ignore information that didn't fit neatly into his rosy outlook on life. Having spent some time in the trenches, I'd come to believe that not everything required positive, big-picture thinking. Sometimes you had to get down in the dirty details and make hard choices.

"Yeah, I'll send the money," I told him.

"Thank you. I'll pay you back in thirty days."

After a couple of years of his never bringing it up, I assumed he wasn't going to pay the money back and wrote it off as a loss.

I still respect my dad immensely. From then on, though, I viewed him through a different lens. My admiration of him took on a broader context. I started to thumb through memories, seeking out the imperfections I had previously ignored. I thought back to the day he had told me he was no longer going to pay for my college. If he was the embodiment of business brilliance, how could he have lost track of his finances like that? I loved him, I admired him, but I started to see him for what he was—a smart and capable but flawed human being who was worthy of respect and admiration, but also not perfect. My dad had shaped my perspectives on faith and business, but had I been following him too blindly? Perhaps the time had come for me to figure things out on my own, to use my own experiences as evidence of how the world worked and identify what *I* felt was most important. I could no longer simply do what my dad told me to do and trust that I would succeed. What followed for me was a major evolution.

Nurtured in part by new doubts about the sacrosanctity of my dad's teachings, seeds of religious doubt that I had harbored for several years began to sprout. The first moment I ever considered questioning the existence of God was in high school. I was sitting in theology class, and the teacher began to describe Pascal's wager, a philosophical argument about the merits of believing in God.

The argument can be depicted as a two-by-two matrix, which the teacher drew on the chalkboard. The columns are labeled "God exists" and "God doesn't exist," while the rows are labeled "Belief" and "Nonbelief." Each box of the matrix represents the outcome for each corresponding scenario. If you believe in God and God exists, then you're set; this is the best possible outcome because it means you'll be welcomed into heaven when your physical body dies. If you believe in God but God doesn't exist, then you're still doing okay. Maybe you don't get to go to heaven or live forever, but you still benefit from the teachings in the Bible. If you don't believe and God doesn't exist, then the outcome is neutral; you aren't rewarded, but you also don't suffer consequences for your disbelief. But if you don't believe in God and you're wrong, then you're in big trouble. I stared at column two: "God does not exist." Up until then, my faith had been so solid that I'd never questioned it. For the first time in my life, I wondered if the faith on which I'd rested my entire sense of purpose was nothing more than fiction.

When doubts entered my mind, I was terrified. The foundation of the two essential aspects of my world—the promise of eternal life and God's unconditional love—started to waver. Immediately, I asked myself a different question: "If all of this is not true, if God does not exist, can I handle it? Would I want to know?" I wrestled with this question throughout the rest of the day, to the point that I couldn't concentrate on anything else. I asked the question over and over until finally I concluded that I would not want to know if God did not exist. I'd based my entire identity and worldview on an unshakable faith in God's existence; to give that up was far too scary and painful to contemplate. "I believe in God," I said to myself, "and if He doesn't actually exist, I don't want to know about it." I tried to put the thought out of my head, but that seed of doubt stayed with me.

The next time the doubt returned, I was in college. Again I was in theology class, and again the teacher displayed Pascal's wager on the board. When I saw the matrix, I immediately thought back to the same question I had asked myself in high school. "Would I want to know if God didn't exist?" I thought about it for several hours, but this time the answer was yes. No matter how painful it would be, if God didn't exist, I wanted to know. I decided I needed to be more committed to reality and truth than to preserving beliefs I'd held since childhood. I thought about my dad's financial woes. I could no longer blindly follow his teachings, and my parents' drive toward independent thought began to overpower the religious doctrine they had instilled in me. I knew right after I made this decision that there was a chance it could be the beginning of the end of my faith as I knew it. This marked a significant turning point for me. It was the first step in a long, difficult journey toward finding my own meaning—with or without God—in life.

7
Tough Choices

IN THE SECOND HALF of 2008, disaster struck. The financial meltdown and ensuing recession hit everyone hard, and Gravity lost 20 percent of its revenue in a matter of months. It wasn't that clients started leaving us; they were just running far fewer transactions. Their customers had started spending less and socking their money away instead of using it to eat out or buy new things. I had a feeling this wasn't something that would pass quickly. My friends, peers, and advisers suggested we lay off employees, cut pay for the employees who remained, and raise our prices to clients in order to protect the company. But any of those decisions would have gone against everything I had set out to build. Those were the tactics employed by the credit card processing companies I wanted to take down. They went so directly against the way I wanted to do business that I knew I couldn't resort to them.

If we didn't change something, however, we were going to go broke in seven months. At the time, we had about thirty-five employees. The typical salary for those on our operations team was around $30,000, and up to that point, I had been trying to give everyone raises of somewhere between 2 and 8 percent each year. At an all-hands meeting, I told the team we wouldn't cut benefits or salaries, but we would freeze all increases in salaries and expenses. "We are going to provide even better support to our clients than in the past," I said. "We will go out and bring on new clients who are looking for the one credit card processor not panicking." I set a goal of getting back to profitability in five months. The team was relieved, although nobody was particularly happy. Everyone got back to work.

In the year before the recession, I had been able to cut back my hours and even take a few days off here and there. Once the recession hit, however, I went back to working eighteen-hour days. After putting in full days at the office, I went door-to-door calling on businesses that accepted credit cards. The recession was taking a toll on the restaurant industry, and I found that many owners who had previously run their restaurants remotely were now getting their hands dirty, since they could no longer afford management staff. This made my sales efforts more effective because the person with the authority to switch processors was often there when I walked in.

Although the work was taxing, our plan worked. Our competitors were jacking up their prices to maintain margins, and this made it easier for us to help new clients save money. Our strategy was not something a CEO could implement from behind a desk. It was only possible with feet on the ground. The miles we were logging started paying dividends.

The minor relief I felt at the early success of our strategy quickly died when I got a call one day from the CEO of our primary vendor, for which we had no backup or replacement. At the time, we were outsourcing part of our technology and banking services, and the vast majority of our clients' credit card transactions were running on this company's software. My relationship with the CEO had been positive since the beginning, and I was happy to hear his voice on the other end of the line. But my warm mood cooled quickly.

"Hey, Dan," the CEO said. Something in his voice told me this was not a social call. "Our sponsor bank is temporarily unwilling to float the interchange." I couldn't believe what I was hearing. Most of the cost associated with any transaction Gravity processes consists of fees charged by the bank that issued the credit card to the consumer. As a result, most of the revenue we earn at Gravity has to be paid out to these different banks. The only problem is that we generally bill our clients at the end of the month. In order to pay the banks throughout the month as the transactions are taking place, we need a sponsor bank to float that money, since it's far more than we would be able to front on our own. Visa, Mastercard, and the other card brands require every credit card processor to have a sponsor bank.

"You need to either pay us the money to float your interchange or, alternatively, you can bill your clients every day," the CEO said. This news spelled death for Gravity. At the time, our monthly interchange was just under $2 million. There was no way we could afford to float that throughout the month. We were having trouble covering our own costs, so we certainly didn't have $2 million to spare. There was also no way we could ask all of our clients to process bills from us every day. Anyone who has done bookkeeping at a small business understands what a disaster this would be. I fumed, but I had few options.

"I'll get back to you," I said. I hung up the phone.

I dropped everything. I poked, prodded, and researched until I discovered that our vendor was in the process of filing for bankruptcy. I remembered that I had received a marketing email from them a few months before. I had received many of these emails in the past, but in this instance, the sender had forgotten to blind-copy the other clients on the message, so all the clients' email addresses were visible to everyone else. I brought up that email and used the information to contact every client. I figured that if we all banded together, we might have a better shot at negotiating. As it turned out, the vendor had approached these other processors with a similar pitch: loan money or die. They all agreed to get on a conference call later that day.

I knew if Gravity tried to fight alone, we would lose. On the call, I asked the CEOs of the other processors if they would fight together with us. We were all competitors, we all had different values and principles, but in that moment, we were aligned against a common enemy. My fellow processors agreed to appoint me as the representative for the unsecured creditors on the bankruptcy committee. I was twenty-four years old.

Based on my own research, I knew the bankruptcy court could potentially allow the vendor to cancel all of the contracts with its clients, including Gravity. This would allow the vendor full access to our client information, with no restrictions on solicitation and lots of leverage, since they controlled the processing infrastructure. Depending on who bought the company, the buyer could legally coerce clients into switching away from Gravity to a higher-margin direct relationship with the buyer. I knew several of the companies getting in line to purchase the vendor were capable of this chicanery. The fight began.

Our attorneys set up a phone line from the Gravity office to the courtroom in Delaware. Back in Seattle, I listened to the proceedings, hanging on the judge's every word. There were three main interests in the process: the senior secured creditors, the second-lien creditors, then the unsecured creditors—Gravity and the other clients of the vendor. The senior secured creditors were in the best position; they would likely get much of the money they were owed. The second lienholders were in a more tenuous position and had a wide range of possible outcomes in the trial. We were in the worst position legally, but prior to the trial, we had allied ourselves with the senior creditors, who had a vested interest in maintaining a working business relationship with Gravity and the vendor's other clients. This move allowed us to achieve essential vendor status, but in doing so, we made enemies of the second lienholders.

I listened as the attorneys battled it out in a war of words.

If the second-lien creditors got their way, Gravity and the other unsecured creditors would get none of the credit card processing revenue the vendor owed us, and our contracts could be canceled. After several days in the courtroom, however, the tide began to turn in our favor. As plans were hashed out, it began to look as though the second-lien creditors might get almost nothing. When the pendulum began to swing farther in that direction, the lead attorney for the second lienholders threw a fit. The judge listened calmly. I knew this was a pivotal moment in the trial: if the judge were to be sympathetic to the attorney's grievances, Gravity could be wiped off the map.

The attorney eventually stopped speaking. After several seconds, the judge acknowledged the attorney's grievances and then asked if she could come up with a better plan. The judge accused the second lienholders of attempting to blow everything up so no one would get anything. The judge refused to adhere to that strategy and announced that he would find the best solution for the most stakeholders. I exhaled a breath I had been holding for too long.

In the end, we found a way to get the vendor to continue operations in bankruptcy and sell the company to an investment group, after fending off several other suitors bent on shutting down operations. Gravity survived, but most important, I was able to keep the promises I had made to our clients. They all continued processing on our system without interruption. They never even knew about the whole episode or how close Gravity had come to collapse.

gave myself a pat on the back for the way I had handled the bankruptcy episode. Our finances were getting stronger, and it looked as if we would be profitable again in a matter of months. The recession was still in full swing, but Gravity was growing out of it. In 2009, my mood improved briefly, but it wasn't long before another threat almost put us out of business for good.

Companies like Gravity assume a significant amount of financial risk. The way the credit card system is set up, the consumer wields most of the power. The old maxim "Let the buyer beware" really doesn't apply when paying with plastic. If a consumer feels she didn't receive the product or service she was supposed to receive, she can call up her credit card company and charge the transaction back, meaning her money is refunded immediately and arbitration ensues. As the company representing the businesses in these cases, we have to ensure that all of our clients are reputable so we don't get stuck with the bill if they don't deliver what their customers paid for. If the client can't pay, we do.

Every single day, we juggle the risk and reward of every transaction that flows through our company. In the depths of the recession, our clients were under insane economic pressure. Many were going out of business. One business owner with a particularly dim financial outlook took matters into his own hands.

One day, just after the bankruptcy fiasco had been put to rest, I walked into work to find a note on my desk from our head of risk, Rosita: "We need to talk." Attached was a letter from one of our clients, a furniture-store owner in Bellevue, Washington. "We are sorry that your furniture has been on back order for the last six months," the letter said. "Unfortunately, we are not going to be able to deliver your order. The good news is that you will get a full refund. To receive your funds, please call your credit card company and issue a charge-back. The bank will then pay you in full."

Rosita and I, along with one of our top risk analysts, Murray, went immediately to try to figure out what was happening to this furniture store. They were supposed to honor all of these charge-backs because they had taken money for orders they never fulfilled, but they could only pay if they had the money, which, it turned out, they didn't. They had declared bankruptcy but had continued taking furniture orders and had used the money to fund other activities. By the time we discovered this, the money from the orders and all of their other assets were gone. We had no chance of collecting anything. The recession and the vendor-bankruptcy crisis had pushed us to the brink ourselves. We had no extra cash lying around, and now we owed $350,000 to cover for this furniture store. At that point, $350,000 represented almost two months of revenue. It looked as though we were finished.

I couldn't believe we had jumped out of the frying pan and into the fire. It didn't seem fair: I had helped so many other companies stay alive, and now I was being screwed by one of the businesses I had worked so hard to protect. With no time to feel sorry for myself, I called a meeting with our risk and underwriting team, led by Rosita.

All of us sat in our only conference room. It was clear we were panicking; we were coming up with no good ideas or potential solutions. We were living in the moment, and the moment was terrifying. We had to change our perspective. Finally, an idea popped into my head. I asked if everyone had seen the TV show *House*, in which an ingenious doctor and his team solve rare medical problems. I got some nods. "Great. Let's pretend we're in that show," I said. "I'll be Dr. House. Rosita, you assign the other roles."

Rosita opted to play a character named Dr. Eric Foreman, Dr. House's trusted colleague. We then went around the room, giving everyone a character to play from the show. The new personas took everyone's mind off the severity of the situation and allowed us to turn our attention away from panicking and toward problem solving. Eventually we dove into our industry regulations—a thousand-page, densely written document that most people avoid cracking at all costs—in an effort to see if there was some rule we could use to our advantage.

After days of scanning the text, we found a technicality in the rules that allowed us twenty days to respond to the card brands for each transaction and make a case for why we shouldn't be responsible for the charge-back. It didn't matter whether our case was strong; we still had twenty days. The bank that issued the card then had ten days to respond back to us and outline their case for why they should not have to cover the losses. If they didn't respond within that time frame, Gravity would win. We realized that if we responded right away, the banks would have more time to write back, so we made sure our responses found their way to the banks on the last possible day, giving them only ten days to respond. We hoped from our experience with big-bank bureaucracy that these Goliath institutions would be completely unable to respond in ten days.

We filled out the relevant forms for every charge-back—of which there were about fifty—and sent the paperwork to the banks on the twentieth day. Each time the bank failed to respond on time, Visa or Mastercard would assess a financial penalty on the bank. Simultaneously, our accounting team went in search of a way to finance the remainder of the losses through a loan from our bank. By the time we were assessed our final penalty, we had the bank financing in place to cover the balance. Once again, we managed to stay alive.

We had survived the bankruptcy of our primary vendor, and we had survived the massive furniture-store fraud incident. With our expenses under lock and key and our entire team working manically, we stayed afloat. By the beginning of 2010, our profit margin was back to 15 percent, close to where it had been prior to the recession. It seemed like a miracle, and although we did celebrate briefly, we couldn't quite shake the paranoia the past few months had engendered. The business was no longer running on fumes, but we didn't change our spending habits. We'd never had as much money as we would've liked in the bank, so we'd always been frugal. I was terrified of running out of cash, and as a result, Gravity and I made money—lots of it. By the end of 2011, our profit margin flew to 35 percent. I was too afraid to give meaningful pay raises in case another disaster struck, and the team was too afraid to ask for them. When I finally came up for air and took stock of the situation, we had a million dollars in the bank and our revenue growth was at 50 percent. What I didn't realize at the time was that this success was coming at the expense of my team and the long-term prospects for Gravity.

8
A New Purpose

AT THE SAME TIME that Gravity was emerging from the recession, my journey with my faith reached a pivotal point. Despite my earlier doubts about the existence of God, I had continued going to Phinney Ridge Lutheran Church in Seattle every week and had even become involved in church operations. I was the church treasurer and an elder, and I led prayers and hymns on Sundays.

But ever since I'd encountered Pascal's wager for a second time, I had started to question my beliefs rather than continue to mold my worldview to fit the doctrine I'd been taught as a child. After college, I had read an essay titled "Dare We Hope for the Salvation of All?" by an Eastern Orthodox bishop named Kallistos Ware. In the essay, Bishop Ware argues that Jesus died for the salvation of all humans, not just Christians. This perspective widened my view of Christianity, and my beliefs became more progressive. I couldn't tolerate the idea that somebody who hadn't done anything wrong, who had just been born in the wrong place or the wrong time or been taught the wrong thing, could be tormented in hell for all eternity. If that was *justice*, then we needed a new definition of the word.

Following one Sunday service at Phinney Ridge in 2007, I approached the pastor, Paul Hoffman, with whom I had become close over the years. I trusted his judgment and respected his understanding of theology. After a brief greeting, I asked him, point-blank, "How do you live with the chance that all of this is untrue? What if it's all just made up? It seems like that's a distinct possibility, don't you think?"

He smiled and waited several seconds before he spoke. "Well, actually, I think that could be right. I have faith that God exists, but I could be wrong."

"What do you mean?" I was shocked at his willingness to acknowledge the possibility that God did not exist. "How can you, as a pastor, stand to live with that belief?"

"Maybe it's just a good analogy for life," he conceded. "Or maybe God is real. I don't know. But either way, I'm happy. I don't spend time worrying whether or not God exists. To me, it doesn't affect the lessons." He gestured to the Bible sitting on the pulpit.

I didn't understand. To Pastor Paul, the truth of God's existence seemed incidental to his faith. For me, faith had always been about two powerful concepts, both of which depended on the existence of God and the literal truth of the Bible. I loved and appreciated many of the moral and ethical teachings of Christianity, but I could learn those lessons without believing in God. The point of religion depended on God's existence, and if God didn't exist, why have faith? Here was an expert who had dedicated his life to Christianity, and even he was open to the possibility that there was an alternative.

I'm not sure what I was looking for from Paul, but I certainly didn't expect what I got. That day in church, I felt my omnipotent creator and eternal life slipping away from me. I felt empty. All of a sudden, life seemed trivial, directionless, and very short. Sure, I was driven by other things like family and work, but without full confidence that God existed, that drive seemed almost trivial. What was the point if there was nothing at the other end? All of humanity would eventually burn up during the next catastrophic cosmic event. There would be nothing left. Life didn't matter, and death was final.

Work was the one thing that could distract me from the void left by my evaporated faith. I allowed it to consume all of my time. I worked long hours, often just to take my mind off things. As long as I was busy growing the company, I didn't have time to think about why I was doing it. I put my head down and lost myself in the work.

Although Gravity still had only about forty employees, the company was catching a lot of attention. In late 2010, I was named the Small Business Association Young Entrepreneur of the Year. I flew to the White House to meet with President Barack Obama and accept the award. I was honored, and the recognition Gravity received further fueled our growth.

Our coffers were filling with cash. I took the award and the influx of money as a sign that we were on the right track. It gave me license to focus even more manically on growing the company. Lucas and I had agreed that I would start drawing a $300,000 annual salary starting in 2008, but once the recession hit, I had stopped taking a paycheck. I cut back my living expenses to the bare necessities and started drawing on my emergency savings to pay for essentials. Starting in 2009, I took a reduced salary, but as we flew into 2011—Gravity having grown 50 percent the previous year—I began taking the full $300,000. Business was good, and our prospects were high. It soon became apparent, however, that not everyone was as upbeat as I was.

As 2011 drew to a close, I started getting feedback—some direct, some indirect—that certain people on our team were unhappy with their pay. Some were more candid about their feelings than others, but essentially people felt that even though they'd played a huge role in helping the company stay afloat through the recession, they were not benefiting from our newfound success. By this point, we had unfrozen wages, but raises were modest—only a few percent annually—and only given out in special cases. I had never stopped to think about what it would be like to work the same long hours I had been working while trying to make ends meet on a stagnant $30,000-a-year salary.

When I first heard about this dissatisfaction, I got defensive. I was very proud of myself for all of the company's recent achievements and successes, and I thought I was doing the right things. I was trying hard to make Gravity successful while still fulfilling our promise to clients and had sacrificed so much of my time, energy, and money to do so. Those sacrifices, I told myself, had been not only for the company but also for our employees. I could have taken the easy way out, as many of our competitors did, and used the recession as an excuse to sell the company or lay off 30 percent of our staff. I could have increased prices to our clients and ended up far wealthier. I could have engineered my way to millionairedom, becoming a twenty-five-year-old with enough money to get by without working for the rest of my life. Instead, I was grinding it out in the trenches every day, and my employees evidently didn't appreciate it.

At the same time, I told myself that if my people were unhappy, they could always leave. Without realizing it, I'd adopted the classic market-driven thinking that a business was only responsible for paying employees enough to stay competitive: anything less than that and they would leave for a higher-paying gig; anything more and I was not upholding my responsibility to maximize profit and minimize expenses. If someone wanted to be paid more, they needed to either take on a new role that would force me to pay them more or look elsewhere for a competing offer.

Frustrated, I started calling friends with business backgrounds and talking to colleagues at Gravity to ask them what they thought I should do. I wanted to see if anyone disagreed with me, but everybody seemed to have the exact same philosophy I did: I wasn't responsible for keeping my employees happy with their pay; I was responsible for running the business profitably. If someone wanted a higher salary, they needed to either find another job or do something that would help me justify paying them more. But the more people I found who agreed with me, the less comfortable I started to feel. I couldn't shake the feeling that something was off. And then I thought about Rosita.

Rosita had started at Gravity in 2006, just after graduating from college with a degree in finance and a mound of student loans. She'd found our job ad on Craigslist and accepted an entry-level position doing data entry and underwriting. Within six months, she started adding more responsibility to her plate, eventually taking over payroll, underwriting, and risk responsibilities and serving as a backup for our support and installation teams. Even then I knew her salary—about $27,000 a year—didn't reflect her contributions to our team, but I didn't realize just how much her low pay was hurting her until much later.

In late 2007, Lucas came to me with some distressing news. Earlier that day, he had been talking to Rosita when he noticed a bright-blue book on her desk emblazoned with the words "McDonald's Crew Trainer Workbook." Was Rosita about to leave Gravity for a management job at McDonald's? If so, what did that say about Gravity as an employer?

We didn't want to jump to conclusions, so we summoned Rosita to Lucas's office. We told her we knew about the training manual and asked her what was going on. She immediately burst into tears. "I'm so sorry," she said. "I didn't want you to find out, but I've been working a second job at McDonald's since April. I need it in order to pay my bills."

After Rosita calmed down, she told us the full story. With her massive student debt, coupled with other huge expenses like rent and a car payment, Rosita literally could not afford to live on her Gravity salary alone. Ten months after she'd started at Gravity, she began working nights and weekends at a McDonald's in Ballard, half an hour's drive from where she lived. Between the two jobs, she was able to eke out a living, but she was also working seventy-five hours a week without any paid time off (at least until we implemented a new PTO policy in early 2008, after which she was entitled to five days of vacation). She hadn't told anyone she was working a second job and had never complained about her financial situation. The training manual had ended up on her desk by accident. McDonald's had just offered her a position as a crew trainer, which would mean more hours but also more money. She'd been told to review the manual before she made a decision and had packed it in her work bag earlier that day. After taking it out while trying to retrieve something else, she had forgotten to put it back. She knew Lucas had to have seen it when he'd come by her desk and was convinced we were going to fire her, which is why she was so upset.

"Rosita, we don't want to fire you," Lucas said, "but we also can't have you working a second full-time job. It's not good for you, and it's not good for the company. What would we need to pay you for you to be able to afford to quit your other job?"

"A lot," she said. "I wouldn't expect you to pay me that much."

"Why don't you go home and figure out exactly how much you need, and then we'll talk," I said. "We want to make this work, and I'm confident we can come up with a solution."

The next day, Rosita told us that if we paid her just north of $37,000 a year, she would be able to cover her most essential expenses. It was a significant increase—roughly 38 percent—but it was worth it to keep a team member like Rosita. From her first day at Gravity, Rosita proved to be one of the hardest-working and savviest people I know. She prided herself on staying busy and learning as much as she could so she could take on more responsibility, serve the team, and grow her own skill set. As disappointed as I was in myself for letting her down, it didn't surprise me at all that she had managed to work a second full-time job without anyone knowing. She was a constant positive presence in the office, and no matter how busy she got, she never seemed stressed. Lucas and I knew that for every dollar we paid her, she would provide ten times that value back to the company.

Lucas, Rosita, and I worked out a plan—in exchange for the raise, Rosita would start taking on more responsibility, which was something she'd been asking for anyway. In addition to her previous responsibilities, she eventually started managing a team of four people and from there grew to be head of our operations department, overseeing our risk, underwriting, and accounting departments as well as our support teams. Today, Rosita oversees our sales training and veterinary sales teams and has proved integral to the growth and sustainability of the company. I'm happy to say she's received many more raises.

In 2011, while discussing my pay policies with others, I remembered Rosita's situation and realized what was bothering me. Without noticing, I had slipped into the business mold I had told myself I was trying to avoid. I had started Gravity with a mission to do something different, to rock the foundation of an industry that wasn't working as efficiently or as responsibly as it could. I'd paved my own path in the credit card processing industry, refusing to accept a given way of doing business just because it was "the way things are done." And yet, here I was, justifying low salaries by pointing to the status quo.

I was making a six-figure salary and hadn't had to scrape by at sub-$40,000 levels for some time. I had assumed that because people weren't jumping ship and the company was growing, we were paying them in line with the job market. The more I thought about the market, however, the more I started to think I was using it as an excuse to put people in objectively bad situations when I had the money to make a difference. We had always put clients first, but was this policy really benefiting them? Who else might secretly be working a second job in an effort to survive? And how could anyone concentrate if they were working all the time and constantly stressed about money? My pay strategy seemed out of sync with the way I had been taught to think about business. It certainly was not a win-win deal.

After stewing on this problem for a while, I determined I couldn't stand idly by any longer. I had to do something to rectify the pain I'd inflicted on my team in the name of frugality. I met with Chloe, our HR manager, to compare notes. She cautioned me to be measured; with the recession still looming large in the rearview mirror, we were all scared of overextending ourselves. We agreed on a $1.00-per-hour across-the-board raise, the most we could afford at the time. More important, we set a goal for that year to average 12 percent raises as a company in an effort to make up for the lost raises during the wage freeze. This was a huge increase from our previous average of 2 to 8 percent. We knew we were going to give up a significant amount of profit, but we felt it would be worth it, just this once, to honor those who had gone through the recession without raises. "Next year, we'll go back to five percent," I said.

I assumed this new plan would be hard on me because it would damage our profit margin, but I was okay with that because I considered it my penance for taking advantage of my team. This self-flagellation—in the form of slower growth—would allow me to cleanse my conscience. I felt terrible about what I had done and wanted to redistribute the rewards of our collective success. For this reason, I was actually looking forward to a reduction in profits. The theoretical value of my share as an owner in the company would decrease due to the unjust way I had been treating the team; the punishment fit the crime.

In 2012, we surpassed our raise goal, and by the end of the

year we had averaged a 26 percent increase in salaries. Most of the people on our support teams were now earning somewhere in the $30,000 to $40,000 range. I was excited to see our team's pay go up so much, but something odd was going on at the same time: our profit margin didn't go down as I had thought it would. It went up. We brought on more clients, and we retained more clients. I couldn't believe my eyes as I looked at a spreadsheet showing our annual salary expenses and our revenue side by side. The lines showing their trajectories were both going up.

We were scheduled to go back to 5 percent raises in 2013 because I hadn't wanted to make promises we could not afford to keep. But here we were with enough money to give the same percentage raises the following year. I knew if I didn't continue the policy, I would find myself once again tormented by the idea that I was hurting my team. In the end, "12 percent average annual raises" was cheerfully placed on our list of goals for 2013. We averaged 19 percent.

A few years earlier, in 2008, Lucas had finally decided to let me buy out his equal share in the company. We agreed to a restructuring, and the company redeemed enough of his shares to give me about two-thirds ownership. We'd grown significantly, and this move resulted in a payout to Lucas of $400,000, which he used to travel the world with his wife. In 2012, Lucas and his wife decided to start a family, so they returned to Seattle.

With no other career to return to, Lucas reengaged with Gravity in his capacity as a board member and shareholder. He asked me to increase the dividends the company was paying to the two of us as shareholders. The fact that a company growing at 30 to 40 percent per year might pay dividends at all was baffling to me; I thought it made far more sense to invest that money back into the company. We began to argue, just as we had in Gravity's early days. When Lucas started to criticize how I was compensating employees, our disagreements deepened.

Every time we saw each other, we inevitably argued, and whatever civility had remained between us quickly evaporated. We couldn't even attend social events without bickering. On one occasion, we attended a Seattle Sounders soccer match, and much to the disapproval of the fans in our section, we spent the entire ninety minutes plus injury time trading shots about dividends, compensation, and finances. Our younger brother Alex had joined us for the game and told us afterward that we both needed to grow up. It was humbling to hear that from a twenty-year-old.

Our falling-out was hard on me. I loved Lucas and wanted to be able to spend time with him without arguing about the company. I received a tie-breaking vote in almost any board decision, since I was the majority shareholder, so I could have easily gotten my way, but I hated the idea that we couldn't come to a compromise. Eventually, I agreed to raise dividends. He agreed to raise my pay.

Fortunately, although our squabbling was emotionally

wrenching for me, it had little effect on the company at that time. It would be several years before everyone at Gravity would be dragged into our feud.

In 2013, our second year of double-digit raises, our profits grew again. I was baffled. At this point, I started wondering if everything I had ever learned about managing payroll (our largest expense) was simply untrue. I began to wonder if our old system of paying market wages was actually inefficient. I thought back to my days of student loans and scraping by to get Gravity off the ground. I remembered how much energy I had spent worrying about money. If money was always at the forefront of people's thoughts, how could they focus on work? By keeping salaries low, had I been inadvertently taking my team's minds off Gravity?

That year, in the business articles and books I was reading, I kept coming across mentions of a study by the behavioral economists Daniel Kahneman and Angus Deaton. As I mentioned at the beginning of this book, Kahneman and Deaton showed that as a person's salary increases to $75,000 a year, their well-being increases along with it. After that point, any increase in salary has an almost nonexistent correlation to increased well-being. The research postulates that this is because, on average, people earning $75,000 are able to afford basic needs as well as some pleasures—like vacations or hobbies. They can lead a comfortable lifestyle free of most financial stress.

Although the average salary of Gravity employees was improving, it was far from $75,000. By keeping people's salaries low and providing little opportunity for financial growth, had I been doing more harm than good? Perhaps there were behavioral economic benefits to our aggressive raises. Was that why our profits had increased in the years we'd implemented them? Or was it just luck and an improving economy?

Before doing anything dire, I decided to try the aggressive pay increases once again in 2014. For the third time, I set my sights on raises of at least 12 percent. You can probably guess what happened: we averaged a 16 percent increase in pay, and our profits shot up again. Throughout my career, I'd been told that in order to stay profitable, businesses needed to keep their expenses, especially payroll, as low as possible. But here we were paying our people much more generously than we ever had while simultaneously becoming more profitable. If the so-called experts had been wrong about this, I wondered, what else might they have missed?

I t was not lost on me that the success of our raise strategy was the result of frontline employees coming forward to question our salary policies. Many business leaders pay lip service to the idea that one person can have an impact. They understand they should solicit and act on feedback from the front lines, but they can't stand the thought of giving up control or putting in the effort it takes to empower others. They trade the expedient "how" for the enduring "why," dictating rather than delegating. This had been my attitude until, through dumb luck, I tasted the success our employees had generated. I wanted more. It was like a sudden, insatiable addiction. I couldn't wait for the next event in which one of my team members would create something or pitch an idea that would inspire a complete transformation at Gravity.

To help satisfy my newfound urge for ubiquitous autonomy, I began spreading an idea throughout the company: "Be your own CEO." I brought up the concept in almost every group meeting and initiated a series of one-on-one meetings to explain it in more detail. The idea was simple: everyone should think of themselves as if they were the CEO of the company. The thinking was that just as CEOs need to hold themselves accountable by considering the consequences of any decision before they make it, every employee should be empowered to do the same. It was about trusting our people to use their best judgment to make decisions and execute on them in a way that would benefit the company. Not only should this allow us to act more quickly and capitalize more fully on the talents of our team, I figured, it should make employees feel empowered to take charge of their own careers and contribute in the way that would make the most sense for them.

We said it to ourselves over and over—"Be your own CEO"— until we all believed that our only mandate was to think and act as if we all controlled the business, our lives, and our futures. We wiped out the acceptability of "because that person told me to do it," in favor of independent thought. With its clear ties to Steven Covey's first habit, "Be proactive," the level of empowerment this mind-set created was amazing. You could see the light in people's eyes when they first truly understood and internalized the fact that they were in control of their professional careers. This attitude worked as a catalyst to the raise schedule. It allowed people the autonomy they needed to add value commensurate with their pay.

We transitioned away from trying to have everything scripted by the CEO, the way five-second plays in a football game are planned in advance. Our work at Gravity became more like a soccer match during which everyone had a general understanding of what we were trying to accomplish but the execution was determined through constant, fluid movement. Once the majority of people at Gravity understood and adopted the "be your own CEO" mentality, our tempo increased rapidly, since people stopped asking for permission. There was no longer a limit to the ideas people could propose or the initiatives they could pursue.

One of the most significant ways the "be your own CEO" concept manifested itself was in the spending of company dollars. We started managing budgets by getting rid of them; the only mandate was to justify every penny. A budget is an arbitrary amount disconnected from the task at hand. By providing a budget, a manager is absolving their team from having to justify expenditures. Whether they spend company money well or poorly, they are in the clear as long as they don't go over budget. The CEO doesn't necessarily have a budget but still has to work within the financial constraints of the company. We made the same rule apply to everyone. This decision further increased employee autonomy and, paradoxically, improved our expense management. People were more careful about spending company dollars when they imagined themselves as the CEO with a finite amount of resources and infinite ways to spend them. Previously, people had come to me and asked how much they could spend on their initiatives, despite the fact that they knew much more about the initiative than I did. I would give them a number, and they would use that as the budget even if it ended up being not enough or more than enough to get the job done. With the new policy, I no longer had to worry about managers spending unnecessarily to max out their budgets. The lack of budgeting forced the decision-making process into the hands of those with the most information and chipped away at unnecessary bureaucracy.

One of my favorite examples of the anti-budget "be your own CEO" philosophy in action related to our office. In 2013, four years before the end of our lease and with the company expanding rapidly, we outgrew our office space. We set out to find a new space and held planning meetings open to anyone in the company to determine the factors they considered important in a new office setup. We aggregated all the data and found a beautiful space: a brand-new empty shell where we would have complete control of the build-out. We enlisted the help of an architect to design a hip new interior that would facilitate communication, provide personal amenities, and generally make life more comfortable for everyone. The space had a view of Puget Sound, a concierge, a marble-floored lobby, and an elevator. We were all excited. We spent several months negotiating the lease with the property developer, and when both parties finally agreed on the contract, we scheduled a meeting so I could sign the papers.

The day of the signing, my team briefed me on several final details. I thought we had done everything possible to involve everyone in the decision. I was happy with the process and ready to move forward. On a whim, I asked to hold an impromptu office-wide meeting. Ten minutes later, I had the entire team in one room. I outlined our plan one last time, even though everyone already knew what I was about to do. I opened the discussion up for questions.

"What's it going to cost?" someone called out.

"We'll pay about four times more than we're paying now—going from about fifteen thousand dollars per month to sixty thousand dollars per month." I continued, jumping at the chance to invoke the "be your own CEO" principle. "At any given point in time, we have a finite amount of resources. If we spend money in one place, we have fewer resources to spend elsewhere. By moving office spaces, we're just taking a little more of our resources and diverting them toward real estate. For the time being, it will decrease the amount we can spend on other things." I was keenly aware of my team's frustrations with our current office space: there wasn't enough desk space or meeting space; we were cramped; parking was limited—the list went on. I was confident that people were excited to move.

"I don't know about you," Alex, our inside sales manager, called out, "but I think if I moved the desks around in my team's room, we could probably fit three or four more work spaces inside." Silence ensued. I stood in front of everyone, not knowing what to say. As it turned out, I didn't have to respond.

"Yeah, I think I could do something similar in our room," a person on our finance team stated.

"Agreed," came another voice.

All of a sudden, there was a flood of solidarity that led to one conclusion: we were staying put. The team had opted against the luxurious office space characteristic of so many tech companies. There would be no kegerators or Ping-Pong tables. We were going to pack it in tight. Looking back, had we made this move, it would have been far more difficult to implement the $70k minimum-wage policy in 2015.

Thanks to the aggressive raises and the concept of "be your own CEO," the company continued to grow. I thought we had stumbled on the perfect formula for business success. We put people on a steep income ramp, while their level of responsibility increased at an even faster rate. This caused our employees to be increasingly underpaid every single year relative to their contributions, but they were making more financial progress overall. It was a professional-development machine that turned out phenomenal people who were making a big impact. Every one of us in a management position started to have conversations internally about how smart we were and about how we had the best compensation philosophy. As long as you were at Gravity, you were going to grow your income quickly. Although our strategy seemed to be working, I still struggled to understand what it all meant.

Gravity's success forced me to double my efforts to fill the void the waning of my faith had left. Work was no longer a distraction from my search for meaning; it was the primary reason for it. I desperately needed to find purpose, and work was increasingly fulfilling that function. I felt Gravity was on a good path toward making credit card processing less evil. We had a long way to go, but we were moving in the right direction. I no longer needed to put in a lot of effort to keep us on track. Helping independent businesses was my ultimate motivator, but now it was the people on the front lines who were primarily carrying the torch.

I was also becoming painfully aware of my new personal financial situation. For my entire life, money had always been short—from my childhood, growing up with five siblings, to the days when I was scraping every penny together to keep Gravity afloat. Now, when I looked at my bank account, I realized I already had enough money to live comfortably for the rest of my life without having to sell the company. When Lucas and I had renegotiated my salary in 2012, we agreed on an $800,000 bonus for me, so along with my $300,000 salary, I made $1.1 million in cash that year. We kept the same arrangement in 2013 and 2014.

Money was no longer a necessity; it was simply a scorecard for gauging my personal success. It was the only metric I had; more profit and more revenue meant I was more successful.

Deep down I knew there was a better way to measure my success, but I didn't know what it could be. When I'd had religion, I would gauge my success based on my relationship with God, but ever since I had begun to doubt my faith, I could no longer rely on that yardstick. Realizing money alone could never fulfill me, I developed an insatiable appetite for the type of inspiration that could bring purpose. I spent hours analyzing my personal life, my professional life, and the large gray area in between. I reread Stephen Covey and thought about the things that mattered to me most. I thought about the business model my dad had taught me of focusing on just helping clients, and about how different the world would be if this simple strategy was more widely adopted.

Based on the teachings of people like Michael Porter, at Harvard Business School, I started to realize that profit was not just a number but a measure of sustainability and scalability. Bigger wasn't necessarily better, but some margin ensured we could grow and make a bigger impact on the independent-business community. Unlike charities, businesses could create a sustainable engine to solve some of the biggest problems facing the world today. This idea was not original. Many thinkers had outlined this concept before, and some businesses had even taken it to heart—Costco, Patagonia, and In-N-Out Burger, to name a few. But these companies were few and far between.

For the first time, I considered the possibility that capitalism could evolve into a vehicle that would transform the world for the better. How could I help that business model take over the economy? I agonized over this question for months until I realized the best thing I could do was set one tiny example.

I didn't develop a one-year goal or even a five-year goal. I eventually settled on a forty-year goal for my professional life. The one thing I cared about above all else was being part of a transformation through which business ceased to be about maximizing profit and started to be about solving the problems facing humanity. Instead of measuring my success against the size of my bank account, I resolved to measure it solely against the impact I had on those around me. I would let my values lead me and let profit follow. If I could succeed in this endeavor, Gravity would be one more example of a company winning with this strategy, and our success would influence others to follow suit. I could help excite a revolution produced by the marriage of capitalism and empathy.

My newfound purpose at once invigorated and terrified me. On the one hand, I'd found the single thing that gave my life meaning again, and I was excited by the opportunities I had before me. In committing to aggressive wage increases for my team, I'd already discovered how bucking convention to do the morally honest thing could pay off. The notion that there might be more I could do by thinking outside the box thrilled me. At the same time, I was faced with a moral dilemma: if I was going to commit to my one true goal, then I had to think even bigger and bolder. I had to do things that no one else had tried before, and I had to be willing to risk everything in order to prove that business could be a force for good in the world. Would I be able to pull it off? Or was this the beginning of the end of my career as a successful entrepreneur?

After I articulated this goal to myself in 2013, everything began to change. Through my newfound ability to connect ordinary tasks—the kinds of things we all have to do to keep the lights on—with my higher purpose and goals, I began to experience a type of magic I'd never experienced before. Every time I convinced a business to use Gravity as their credit card processor, I was demonstrating to the world how we could be successful by focusing on helping that business, rather than on the profit we would make from them.

When I first settled on this goal, it sounded so grand as to be absurd. How could I possibly have the type of impact I dreamed about? How could I, one guy from Idaho, possibly effect change in the way people did business? But once I knew this was the one thing for which I would give up everything else, the world fell into place for me. I had a blueprint for success, but it took more than two years for me to learn what it really meant to translate that goal into action.

9

Distraction

I HAD MY GOAL. I knew where I was going, but I was constantly distracted. I was still scared of what had happened during the recession, and I used that fear to justify greed. Instead of simply focusing on my one goal—to put purpose ahead of profit—I found myself hoarding cash in the name of financial security. My salary continued to increase, and my bank-account balance soared. Watching the numbers rise reinforced for me the way I was running the business. If we were making money, I must be doing the right things.

Meanwhile, I was managing a huge change in my personal life. Kristie and I had been together for eleven years—married six—but in the fall of 2011, we decided to separate. We still loved one another deeply, but a few years into our marriage it became clear that our original reasons for getting married no longer applied. Our religious beliefs had evolved, and so had we. Living in Seattle had exposed us to people, attitudes, and lifestyles we'd never encountered growing up in Idaho, and we began to wonder whether staying together was preventing us from fully growing into the individuals we were becoming.

In the time we'd been together, Kristie had started blogging and journaling, and she turned to writing to help her process the end of our marriage. She wrote a letter to me and our close friends and family in which she explained her feelings about our decision to separate. In it, she perfectly summed up our relationship: "Two friends, forever changed, no longer husband and wife."

Kristie moved to San Francisco, and we mutually agreed on a settlement we both considered fair. I didn't hire a lawyer for the divorce, and Kristie was careful not to ask for anything that would have jeopardized Gravity. When she moved, she left behind her nine-year-old rescue dog Mikey, whom she had adopted a few years prior. Although Mikey had always lived with both of us, and he'd become extremely important to me, there was never any question that he was Kristie's dog. Kristie told me she'd come back to get him after she got settled in California, and I steeled myself at the thought of saying goodbye. Mikey was the closest thing Kristie and I had to a child, and he provided such comfort and love to both of us. I would never have asked to keep him, but I didn't want to lose him either.

A few weeks after Kristie moved, I emailed her asking if she could give me plenty of notice before she came to pick Mikey up so I could prepare. She wrote back to say that she thought it might be in my and Mikey's best interests for him to stay with me, so he did. Kristie and I stayed in touch and saw each other a few times after our divorce was finalized in early 2012, but for the most part we gave each other the space to lead separate lives.

N ewly wealthy and single for the first time since high school, my lifestyle began to evolve. The transition began accidentally and was slow at first. Back in 2008, I had been introduced to a few successful executives by way of my membership in the Entrepreneurs' Organization, a networking group for business owners. Through those connections, I had been invited to upscale parties, posh trips to Vegas, six-figure card games, and five-figure dinners. Over time, these occasions became a bigger and bigger part of my social life. By 2014, I was cavorting with the Seattle business elites, helicopter skiing at exclusive luxury resorts in British Columbia, and attracting my fair share of attention from women. It was far and away beyond anything I ever could have imagined while growing up in rural Idaho.

As a young, rising CEO in the Seattle tech scene, I found that a new group of people began to take notice of me. My circle of friends was increasingly filled with CEOs, successful entrepreneurs, and other well-to-do leaders. Most were worth tens or even hundreds of millions of dollars. They had invested in Amazon back in 1999, cashed out of Microsoft to go start their own companies, or simply started from scratch and been wildly successful. Every business or social event I attended seemed to bring me further into this circle.

As a junior member of this posse of winners, I looked on with wonder at the strange displays of excess that accompanied their wealth. I played poker with pots the size of two starting annual salaries at Gravity. Once, I watched a friend lose $250,000 in a day trade while his leftovers were reheating in the microwave. One evening, a handful of my CEO peers spent $2,000 to rent a private room in a high-end restaurant. As if we hadn't already racked up enough of a bill on lobster tail and Wagyu beef, one of the attendees smashed two bottles of Dom Pérignon on the antique dining table. To this day, I'm still not sure how much he had to pay for the damage. On another occasion, a friend left his car in the airport pickup zone because he was late for a flight. He had his assistant pick up the vehicle from the impound and told me the price of this makeshift valet-parking job was worth it; he did make his flight after all.

It was as if the man in the suit had allowed me to pass through the velvet rope into a seductive and exclusive world. I didn't know what to do. It felt great and wrong all at once. I couldn't invite other friends to these events because none of them could afford the entry fees or dinner tabs. As a result, friends I had made back in college and high school began to take a back seat. I didn't necessarily enjoy spending time with one group over the other; the shift just happened naturally. Every event I attended led to more introductions, which led to more invitations. Soon my calendar was packed with executive networking events, fancy dinner parties, and private flights to exotic locales.

In addition to the expensive trips and dinners, I began to get a lot more attention from women. Could I attribute my newfound appeal to wealth? It was an ugly thought that I initially dismissed with justifications and excuses. I may have doubted the existence of God, but Christianity was in my blood. The idea of succumbing to this new temptation was unthinkable, but it wasn't long before prudence gave way to pleasure. I began dating models, NFL cheerleaders, and local celebrities. It was so easy. Beautiful women wanted to introduce me to their friends, and sometimes they would all find their way back to my house. As my friends would sometimes remind me when I expressed misgivings about my new lifestyle, I was living every man's fantasy. Intellectually I knew the private jets, the thousand-dollar bottles of wine, and the attractive women shouldn't matter. But in practice, I found I simply could not resist the temptation. The money followed me wherever I went. Who was going to tell me to stop?

My faith had transformed into something far more flexible. My life's purpose was no longer guided by God. I looked to my forty-year goal for direction, but in reality I just kept finding ways to fit that goal to my actions. I pointed to the clients we were helping and the raises we were providing to employees as evidence that I was progressing. It took quite a bit of this fast-paced lifestyle before I stopped to ask myself how much more progress I could be making. I had told myself that I would sacrifice anything for my one goal, but my lifestyle didn't match my words.

This incongruity was exacerbated by increased notoriety and exposure. That year, I was named *Entrepreneur* magazine's Entrepreneur of 2014. I figured the feature on me would consist of a small blurb relegated to page 50 of the magazine, but when the issue hit shelves, I received a text message from a friend. The message contained no words, just a picture of a magazine stand in an airport bookstore. Confused, I expanded the picture and zoomed in for a closer look. There, sandwiched between *Fast Company* and *Inc.*, was my picture, taking up the entire *Entrepreneur* cover. I was in total shock.

After hearing the news, I immediately called my dad, Ron. Even though I hadn't openly discussed with him my mission to lead a business revolution, we had often talked about the importance of purpose and morality in leadership. He also knew the lifestyle I was living and was always worried about the effects fame and fortune might be having on me. I picked up the phone, and after a short greeting, he got right to the point.

"Dan, I'm proud of you," he said. I could tell from his voice there was going to be a big caveat. "But this is a character test. However strong your character was yesterday—whatever amount of integrity, strength, and courage it took to get to where you are right now—that level of strength will not be adequate in the future. You will experience new tests. You will have extra attention on you, extra power, and extra access to all things.

There will be new, tougher standards. Are you prepared?"

When I didn't answer, he continued.

"You need to be absolutely certain about two things: you

need to understand who you are, and you need to know where you are going. With this latest success, you are going to be blitzed with attention, and more and more people will be trying to knock you off your path." I felt anxious, but then he put me at ease: "Your mom and I love you, and we're so proud of you."

Not sure how to respond, I changed the subject and asked for updates on the rest of the family. Shortly after that, I said goodbye and hung up the phone.

I knew he was right. My dad was proud, but he was more concerned with my future and my integrity than he was with my fame. While I was still reeling from this newfound notoriety, Ron had already moved on to preparing me for the next stage of the journey. That short call made an impression on me. It deepened my desire to focus on my one professional goal. I began to think harder about what I would need to change or improve upon to pass the next character test, whatever that might be.

10

The Decision

IN THE BEGINNING OF 2015, we were teeing off for another year of 15 percent raises. We had averaged 20 percent wage increases for the last three years, the company was growing, the team was becoming more entrepreneurial, and I had begun to refocus my faith toward a more earthly purpose. I was feeling very proud of myself. I felt like we had figured out some hidden secret to organic growth—but something still didn't sit quite right with me. We were investing a lot in our team, but they were giving back much more.

Philosophically, what I wanted to create at Gravity was a place where people could come to work and pretend they were volunteers. I had implemented our raise policy because I didn't want my people to have to worry about money, and I also didn't want money to be the only reason they came to work. We had non–compensation-related policies that supported this view, such as an open-paid-time-off policy that allowed all employees to arrange their own vacation schedules with their managers, but the salary structure didn't fit. Despite the raises, people were still very conscious of their pay. A third of the company was still making less than $40,000, and entry-level salaries were in the low thirties. This didn't seem tenable.

Specifically, I couldn't figure out how this pay structure would get us to our next phase of growth. Our first thousand clients had my cell phone number. As a result, I could oversee every interaction our team had with them. But that model had become unsustainable. I had to trust everyone at Gravity to do the right thing, take full responsibility, and make strategic decisions. How could someone making $30,000 a year in Seattle—which, in 2015, ranked as the city with the eighth-highest rent in America— do anything but live paycheck to paycheck?[4] They had to be worried about money, yet I was entrusting them to set their own financial concerns aside to focus on those of our clients. Meanwhile, I was increasingly conscious of my million-dollar salary. The discrepancy didn't feel right, but I was able to live with cognitive dissonance for a while in the absence of fresh ideas. Around this time, I took my fateful hike with Valerie.

That day on our hike, I realized how much I could still sacrifice in order to achieve my lifelong goal. I was living a life of luxury when some members of the Gravity team were struggling to make ends meet. How was that an example of a values-based company? If Gravity succeeded with its current pay structure, it would never be the example I hoped it would serve as. All of our

---

4. Andrew Woo, "December 2015 Apartment List National Rent Report," Apartment List, January 4, 2016, apartmentlist.com/rentonomics/december-2015-apartment list-national-rent-report/.

success would have been at the expense of the frontline employees who were doing the most to help our clients. It wasn't fair, and it certainly didn't support my long-term goal to usher in a new era of business. If being an example of a successful values-based company was really the thing I cared about more than anything else in my professional life, then I needed to bring all of my own resources to bear.

When I decided to take a day off work to hike with Valerie, I had no idea I would be returning to my car with a plan that would transform the lives of not only the team at Gravity but also many other people around the world. By the time I had finished the hike and kicked off my boots, I had worked out the core of my plan. I knew our financial position well enough to know approximately what we could afford. I would raise the salaries of my lowest-paid employees immediately to at least $50,000. In two years, I would make sure everyone in the company was at or above $70,000. This was what we could afford, and although it wouldn't get everyone to Kahneman and Deaton's $75,000, it would be close.

All told, the move would cost us roughly $2 million a year— pretty much all of Gravity's annual profit. I couldn't risk leaving the company without a financial buffer, so I decided to reduce my salary from $1.1 million to $70,000 in order to help offset the cost. I had enough money in the bank that I wouldn't have to change my lifestyle too much, and it was worth sacrificing money I didn't strictly need to help improve my employees' lives. Plus, I was optimistic that, if we were successful, we'd quickly make up the difference in profit and I'd eventually be able to increase my salary again.

After the initial excitement of my plan wore off, doubts surfaced. Throughout the two weeks following the hike, I experienced a roller coaster of emotions. One day, I would be overcome with joy at the thought of what I was about to do; the next, I would sink into a black hole of doubt and despair. I woke up every night with terrors. I told myself to forget this plan. I thought about how great my life was. I thought about how much money I was making and the number of jobs we had created. I thought about how successful Gravity was financially. I told myself that changing this beautiful status quo was a terrible decision.

Then I thought back to what my dad had said. Was this the character test he had warned me about? Was I actually prepared to give up stability and comfort for my beliefs—my one goal? Old habits die hard, and despite my evolving faith, one verse from the Bible, written by James, the brother of Jesus, played over and over in my head: "Knowing the right thing to do and not doing it is sin." I tried to interpret this verse in any way other than its literal meaning. I couldn't. There was no escaping the conviction that implementing the $70k minimum wage was the right thing to do for the people at Gravity—and for me— and not doing so was just as wrong as stealing.

Before making the final decision, I wanted to run the idea by others. I chatted with about twenty other CEOs, half of whom were Gravity clients and half of whom were not. It was important for me to speak with them because Gravity's whole business is about serving other businesses. I thought the $70k wage policy might hurt other businesses that didn't have the same means because it might make them look bad. By not following suit, would they be seen as implicitly standing up against a living wage? The last thing I wanted to do was hurt the businesses I was trying to help.

I had long, intimate conversations, but the message was very consistent. The typical response was, "Okay, Dan, you're crazy. I would never have dreamed up something like this. But you've pulled off a lot of this wild shit in the past. Maybe you can pull this off, too."

After vetting the idea with other business leaders, I took my plan internal. I talked to almost everyone at Gravity who was responsible for setting our compensation levels. In addition, I had conversations with our financial team. On the back of a napkin, I had determined that the program would add about $1.8 million to our annual payroll, but I wanted my work double-checked. "Can we afford it?" I asked.

"Barely," was the response.

Finally, I spoke to Ryan, our marketing director at Gravity. He thought this could be an interesting news story and began making calls to a couple of media outlets. After speaking with him, I wondered if we could pay for a small percentage of the increased expenditure by generating awareness for the company. Maybe some businesses would hear about our values and how we operated and want to work with us. There was just one problem: no media outlet was interested. The pay raises would have to pencil out without any publicity.

After the press turned me down, I started to think more philosophically about the decision. Our clients were obviously essential, since they pay our salaries. Some quick math led me to conclude that raising our minimum salary would cost about $10 per client per month. It wasn't as if any of our clients would be charged higher rates; it was just a reallocation of our profit, but I still wondered if I could justify it. "What if I just gave each client $10 off their credit card processing every month? Perhaps the money would be better spent that way?" It seemed like a tiny amount, but for independent businesses running tight margins, every penny helps. I started Gravity to serve these businesses, so I had to think hard about this question. Would our clients benefit more from higher-paid support personnel or from $10 extra per month? I eventually came to the conclusion that it would be better for our clients to be interacting with people who were being paid a living wage and who had less stress. In addition, if our employees could afford a middle-class lifestyle, they would be able to spend more of their money at our clients' businesses.

After deciding that the wage increase was worth $10 per client, my mind drifted further into the abstract. "What if I didn't have the money to give my team this raise? What if my finance team had come back with a spreadsheet that showed a dimmer outlook?" I had already determined that the $10 per month was better spent in the hands of my team. Would I have been willing to raise prices to make the new minimum-wage policy work? I quickly put the thought out of my head, determining I probably didn't have the guts to make that decision and hopefully wouldn't need to.

Finally, several days before the scheduled announcement, we received a reply from the *New York Times*. The reporter we'd pitched wasn't interested in the story but agreed to make an introduction to someone else at the paper. Eventually Ryan connected with Patricia Cohen, an established business writer, who agreed to write a short story about our impending policy shift.

The same day we were connected with Patricia, we heard from Joe Fryer, who had previously covered us as a reporter for King 5, Seattle's NBC affiliate. Joe had since been promoted to a producer position at *NBC Nightly News* and *Today*. After discovering this, Ryan had immediately reached out to him. Joe said he didn't think anyone would be interested, but he agreed to check with his senior editor. We didn't have high hopes, but hours later we received a call. "We got the go-ahead," Joe said. I couldn't believe it. I was going to appear on *NBC Nightly News*, one of the most popular and respected evening news programs in the country. After getting no traction for weeks, we had two of the biggest media outlets in the country poised to tell our story.

I did a quick Google search and some math. It looked like *NBC Nightly News* had about eight million viewers per night.

The *New York Times* had a circulation of around one million people, plus an unpredictable yet massive online presence. I picked the round number of ten million as the likely total audience for the announcement. If we got a response rate of two in ten thousand, two thousand people would engage with Gravity in some way. If you estimate that one out of every ten people who engaged with us would present a business opportunity, that's two hundred new prospective clients. If we made $200,000 from those clients, it would cover one-tenth of the cost of the raises.

As it turned out, I grossly underestimated the situation. I had no idea how much dormant energy existed around this issue. Looking back, nothing could have prepared us for the storm that followed.

I decided to announce our new pay policy at our quarterly meeting in April 2015. There were about fifty people attending by teleconference and about eighty in the room at our main office. I took some quiet time to myself before making the announcement. I was happy, I was nervous, I was looking forward to no longer holding this in. I wanted this weight off my shoulders.

Just before the end of the meeting, I took a deep breath and said, "For the last twelve years, we've dedicated ourselves to helping one business owner at a time. We're in love with independent businesses—the way they influence our communities and the way they help us—and we want to keep serving them. In my mind, there's a major threat to them, which is growing inequality. This is an issue that is very personal for me, and it impacts the people we care about—those business owners. They are dependent on a strong middle class to succeed. Also, if I look at our team members today, a lot of folks on the teams that are close to our clients, their starting pay range is between thirty thousand and forty thousand dollars a year. I feel guilty about that because I think to really survive in Seattle, you need to make a minimum of forty thousand dollars a year. And I think to really thrive you have to make seventy thousand dollars per year. So what I wanted to announce today is, effective immediately, we're going to put a scaled policy into place, and we're going to have a minimum pay rate of seventy thousand dollars for everyone who works here."

After I finished, there was an awkward silence. The news clearly hadn't sunk in. I was surprised. I had been thinking so much about this policy for the last three weeks, I expected everyone to process it instantly. Finally, someone asked me to repeat the announcement, so I went through it all again. When I finished, there was more silence.

Just under a third of the people in the room were getting their pay doubled, a little more than a third were getting significant but less substantial raises, and a third were already earning at least $70,000, so their salaries would stay the same. Luckily, after an eternity of silence, Garret, an outside sales rep who was in town for the company meeting, started screaming.

Then everyone started screaming and clapping. The mood changed from one of uncertainty to one of ecstasy. Everybody felt it. Some people later expressed unhappiness and discomfort with the decision because they didn't think it was fair to more experienced employees or they worried what our clients would think. But in that moment, everybody was equally euphoric. It was amazing. It was such a fun, happy moment for our team to share.

I didn't know this at the time, but Garret, who had initiated the screaming, had one single goal in life: to live until he was forty-five, so he could see his youngest daughter graduate from high school. At the time of the announcement, he was thirty and had already outlived his dad, who had died at thirty from cancer. To meet his goal, he had to come close to outliving his mom, who had died from cancer at age fifty. He was living with a genetic curse and had taken a 50 percent pay cut to come to Gravity after working in a factory doing a type of welding known to cause cancer. The new policy meant he no longer had to make a financial trade-off in order to protect his health.

After Garret, others joined in. There were high fives all around the room. To this day, I cannot imagine being any happier than I was at that moment. Nydelis, a member of our risk management team, immediately cornered me. Nydelis was born in Puerto Rico and moved to the United States when she was six. She had been making $36,000, which was more than either of her parents had ever made. She told me, "Dan, I have one dream in life right now. I was so happy to be making what

I was making and so proud of my job. I wanted to be able to fly my parents out to Seattle and show them the life I've built for myself. As the first person in my family to go to college, I have thousands of dollars in student loans. Yesterday I couldn't figure out how I was going to pencil everything out to pay off these loans and realize my dream. Today, everything has changed."

Later Cody, who worked on our support team, said he and his wife had been holding off on starting a family—the most important dream they had—until they could pay down their debt. Cody had studied his budget closely and immediately knew the impact this raise would have: he and his wife would be able to pay down their debt and start their family several months earlier than they had anticipated. Cody is not always an outwardly emotional person, but hearing his story brought me close to tears. The atmosphere was truly indescribable. I was still feeling happier than I had ever been before. We all went across the street to a local brewery (a Gravity client) to celebrate. I walked around and spoke with as many people as I could. I heard the most amazing feedback. For the first time, the team was telling me their stories and, more importantly, how those stories were about to change. Then I got a tap on the shoulder.

I had been so nervous about the policy shift and the announcement that it felt good to relax after the meeting. People were excited, but I had already moved on to thinking about running Gravity under this new policy. Just as I started to think it was time to get back to work, somebody let me know the *New York Times* article was live. An hour later, I got a text from a friend that read, "Dan, there's a story about you that's number one on Hacker News." I had never heard of Hacker News, but I quickly learned it was a popular trending-news site. An hour after that, I got an email: "Dan, there's a story about you that's number one on Reddit right now." I didn't know what Reddit was either.

The next day, starting at 4:00 a.m., I began receiving so many calls that my cell phone stopped working. They were from ABC, NBC, CBS, CNN, Newscorp—most of the major media companies in the world—each of which was calling to request an interview. At this point, the *New York Times* story had been picked up or written about in media markets across the globe. Hundreds of thousands of visitors started bombarding our website.

We got so many media requests that I ended up having to fly to New York for a whirlwind press tour. NBC sent a producer to accompany me on the flight from Seattle because they said they were worried I might get intercepted by ABC or CBS, which had also booked me for interviews. I appeared on *NBC Nightly News* that evening, as planned, before my appearance on *Today* the following morning.

After *Today*, I was called back into the *NBC Nightly News* studios to do a one-on-one interview with Lester Holt. I also appeared on *CBS Evening News* and ABC's *World News Tonight* that evening before appearing on all three network morning shows the following day. It was a crazy few days, and my phone never stopped ringing, but I was happy because I knew I had struck a chord. Not only was the $70k decision the right thing to do for Gravity, but it was proving to be a major step toward my goal of influencing other businesses by championing purpose-driven leadership. I felt as if I were truly sending the message that business could be a force for good rather than an engine for profit and an outlet for greed. And I was doing it in a way that felt right and honest to me.

B ack at the office, our business was transforming. A trickle of inbound activity turned into a river, just before it became an all-out flood. Our general-contact email address, which had previously received about ten messages per day, started receiving thousands of messages. In the hours after the news broke, we received about one email every ten seconds. The vast majority of these correspondents were well-wishers, supporters, or critics, but some of the emails were from business owners inquiring about Gravity's services. The few people who were generally responsible for answering these emails were spending all of their time taking care of the phones. For the first time in our history, we were forcing people to wait on hold. To fix this, the team sprang into action. People from all departments were pressed into customer service. Even our lawyer began taking calls and answering emails. One hundred and twenty Gravity employees went into overdrive.

Potential clients and commentators were not the only ones

who reached out to us. As you can imagine, the new salary increase attracted résumés—lots of them. Our recruiting team was completely overwhelmed. We received seven thousand résumés in the first week after the announcement, and our system was not set up to handle anything close to this level of activity. We implemented a screening process to weed out those who hadn't put effort into their applications, but even with these controls, the applications kept coming. Anyone who wasn't answering phones or emails started sorting job applications. We were only hiring for a couple positions, but we wanted to make sure we didn't miss any opportunities to bring on talented people.

While our traditional contact points were being inundated, our social-media sites were getting blasted, too. Thousands of interactions turned into millions. The story of Gravity Payments remained a trending topic on major sites like Facebook, Twitter, Buzzfeed, and Reddit for several days. Patricia Cohen's story about us was the most-read article on New York Times's website. More and more people were discovering the story and were interacting with it. NBC's Joe Fryer told us that the online video of NBC's story on the announcement became the most viral video in their history at the time. Inbound messages came in every form. I think back to those few days and cringe at the opportunities we missed: we were so focused on running the business, we even accidentally blew off the US secretary of labor, Tom Perez, who called the company's main line and asked to speak with me.

I also received a lot of messages on my personal LinkedIn page from people who wanted to work with Gravity. One came from a woman named Tammi Kroll, the VP of production operations at Yahoo. Thankfully, my friend and colleague Chloe on our HR team was monitoring my inbox and alerted me to Tammi's message. Tammi was going to be in Seattle and wanted to meet. I assumed she was going to be in town on business, or maybe to visit friends or family in the area. I thought maybe I could convince her to try to implement some type of new compensation program at Yahoo. The opportunity to speak with someone so high up at one of the world's major tech companies excited me.

When Tammi arrived at the Gravity office a few days later, I introduced myself and we walked across the street to Top Pot, a local coffee and doughnut shop. We discussed our various business experiences and philosophies, and I was immediately impressed. She was so smart and so humble. She had worked her way up from an entry-level programming position at a financial-services company to become the person responsible for overseeing Yahoo's entire technology and applications infrastructure.

But Tammi was not only driven in her own development; she was driven to serve others. Years before, at one of her previous jobs, she had been promoted to the executive level and was poised to receive her first big bonus check. Just before the money was dispersed, the company announced a round of layoffs. Uncomfortable with the fact that some people were getting bonuses while others were losing their jobs, she ran some numbers and determined that if all the executives gave up their bonuses, 10 percent of the people who were set to be laid off could keep their jobs. She took her proposal to the executive team and was laughed out of the boardroom. It was clear to me that this experience had been weighing on her for a long time. She was exactly the opposite of the flashy, spoiled Silicon Valley executive stereotype. I was honored to have the chance to get to know her, even if it was just over coffee.

At one point, I asked Tammi where she saw herself in the next ten years. After giving it some thought, she said she'd like to have a hybrid role at a "smaller" company where she could leverage her background in development and operations.

"What do you mean by 'smaller company?'" I asked.

"One with about five thousand people," she said.

I laughed and told her five thousand people was hardly a small company but that the role she described sounded interesting. I joked that if only we could afford her, I'd love to have her come work in that role at Gravity. I knew we could never pay her anything close to what she was worth, but the fact that Tammi didn't immediately laugh off the idea struck me as yet another sign that she was special.

As we started to say our goodbyes, I asked Tammi where she was heading next.

"The airport," she said.

I was confused. "I thought you came from the airport?"

"I did."

"Aren't you here on business or to see friends or something?"

"No." She smiled.

"So . . . why did you come to Seattle?"

"I came to meet you."

I felt bad that I had just squeezed this meeting in between several other appointments that day. If I'd known she made the trip solely to see me, I would've cleared my calendar to make it worth Tammi's time. I asked her to stay longer. "No, I know you're busy. I'm headed back. Thank you for your time, and let me know if you want to talk later." We shook hands, and she left.

Over the next few weeks, Tammi and I stayed in touch and even had the opportunity to meet face-to-face a couple of times when I was in San Francisco on business. I found out later that Tammi had been thinking about her next career move and, after the $70k announcement, was considering coming to work for Gravity. Eventually our conversation turned to what her role with us might look like, but as excited as I was by the prospect of having her on our team, I started to feel guilty at the idea of what she'd be giving up. Not only would she sacrifice most of her compensation, she'd be leading a team barely a fraction of the size of what she was used to. Tammi had worked her way up to become a hugely successful woman in an industry that is notoriously unkind to women, and she was thinking about walking away from it all? The idea was so absurd to me that I didn't even know how to make her an offer that wasn't insulting.

After several more weeks of conversation, Tammi accepted

our offer to come work at Gravity. She would serve in a combination of chief officer roles—in operations, technology, and information—and she'd oversee all of our operations teams, which at the time amounted to fewer than one hundred people. In late summer of 2015, just before Tammi's first day at the company, I called her up. "How am I supposed to feel comfortable with the fact that you're essentially volunteering your time in a for-profit organization?" I asked. "You're making what amounts to a seven-figure donation every year you work at Gravity."

"Dan, it is worth it to be at Gravity," she said. "I'm willing to sacrifice the money." She retold the story of the layoffs and bonuses. Since that moment, she'd been harboring a sense of guilt and a desire to be part of something bigger, something more meaningful. I felt the weight of her sacrifice on my shoulders. It was the same weight I had felt when I first hired David Meissner at $24,000 a year with no benefits. It was the same weight I had felt when Matt Sakauye quit his job and took a pay cut to work at Gravity. Money wasn't going to make this a good opportunity. I just didn't have that luxury. I had to come up with something else.

"Okay, Tammi. We can do this, but I'm going to do everything I can to make sure that this is a good decision for you. I don't know how I could have any chance of doing it, but I'm going to try."

She shrugged off my commitment as unnecessary, but I felt it was my responsibility to keep my promise.

Tammi was not the only person who offered to leave a large sum of money on the table in order to work with Gravity. Other executives reached out and made similar proposals. As I took each of these meetings, I couldn't help but feel the tide was turning. The craving these highly paid individuals had to be a part of something money could never buy made me feel that the sun was starting to set on an era of moneymaking for moneymaking's sake. I thought back to my goal to lead a business that focused on solving problems rather than just making money. With the new microphone I had been given and the clear groundswell of change that was taking place around Gravity, I realized I could now do even more in support of my mission. I grabbed the microphone and began to tell anyone who would listen about the transformation I was witnessing.

11
Backlash

THE DAY AFTER THE $70K ANNOUNCEMENT, I received a text message from my parents. They were listening to the voice of my childhood, Rush Limbaugh, who had announced his intention to discuss Gravity's new policy later that day on his program. My parents were proud and excited that I would be featured on a show they had listened to for decades. As the segment on Gravity began, however, their excitement quickly dissipated.

Rush lambasted my decision. He assured his fans that Gravity would fail and become a high-profile example of how to destroy a successful company. "This is pure, unadulterated socialism, which has never worked," he said. "That's why I hope this company is a case study in MBA programs on how socialism does not work, because it's gonna fail . . . and . . . it isn't gonna take long because once everybody figures out they're all making the same, no matter what they do, the slackers are gonna surface. Human nature!"

Although I disagreed with everything Rush said and he misrepresented our policy by saying everyone would be making the same salary, the experience was a wake-up call for me. I'd always thought conservatives like Rush believed in the power of the private sector to fix society's ills. What was wrong with a private business owner making a decision about how to run his company in the way he saw fit? For the first time, I realized there were people out there who would actively try to undermine what we were trying to accomplish at Gravity. Rush became the original enemy of the $70k minimum wage.

My parents were disappointed. They were proud of my moral stance and how it aligned with some of the most fundamental teachings of the Bible, like Luke 3:11: "Anyone who has two shirts should share with the one who has none, and anyone who has food should do the same." Or Proverbs 11:24–25: "One person gives freely, yet gains even more; another withholds unduly, but comes to poverty. A generous person will prosper; whoever refreshes others will be refreshed." They didn't like the fact that a media personality whom they had so long admired was enacting a scorched-earth policy toward my decision making. "Rush got it wrong this time," my dad said on the phone with me after the show. "He just doesn't have all the facts. He's busy and wasn't able to investigate the move thoroughly."

I smiled on the other end of the line. Over the years, I'd come to see the holes in Limbaugh's logic, so I wasn't all that surprised he got this wrong, but I decided I could save that conversation with my parents for another time. Rush Limbaugh says I'm a radical, but I see his version of capitalism—one in which corporations should not be held accountable for the harm they cause (consciously or not) to society—as much more radical. In fact, I find it dangerous. We live in a time in which corporate greed can be blamed for everything from massive income inequality to the decline in public health to catastrophic climate change, and yet people should fear *me* because I choose to pay my employees a living wage?

Despite my break with Rush's extreme ideology, he was right about a couple of things. Not everyone at Gravity was as pleased by the new minimum wage as I'd assumed they would be. Two key employees decided to leave as a result of my decision. One left because she didn't think it was fair that she and others had had to work their way up to the $70k threshold over the course of many years while those who were new to their roles escaped that fate. She later spoke out about my decision, saying that I "gave raises to people who have the least skills and are the least equipped to do the job, and the ones who were taking on the most didn't get much of a bump." The second employee didn't like the fact that his pay was now the same as the pay of those he saw as adding less value to the company and who weren't working as hard as he was. He also spoke out against the decision. "Now the people who were just clocking in and out were making the same as me. It shackles high performers to less motivated team members."

A few journalists compared the decisions of these employees to those of the field workers in the parable told in Matthew 20:1–16. In the story, a wealthy landowner hires day-wage laborers in the morning to work on a vineyard. The landowner goes out again in the afternoon and hires more workers. He decides to pay these new workers the same amount as those hired in the morning, even though they would work fewer hours. The laborers who worked the entire day begin to complain, despite being paid their agreed-upon salary. In response, the landowner replies, "I am not being unfair to you, friend. Didn't you agree to work for a denarius? Take your pay and go. I want to give the one who was hired last the same as I gave you. Don't I have the right to do what I want with my own money? Or are you envious because I am generous?"

This metaphor may be convenient, but it's not entirely accurate to our story. We weren't paying everyone an equal wage, and in setting a minimum salary, I wasn't trying to be generous. Besides, sometimes you need to do things that might be considered "unfair" in order to make progress. Shouldn't we come down on the side of making things better for the most people rather than making sure only certain people are happy?

Many agreed with this perspective, but the challenges kept coming. "The pay increase is foolish," wrote one commentator in an online journal. Another blogger compared Gravity to a sinking ship after narrating a history of failed communist experiments. More moderate critics predicted a slow, steady demise or a move that would only work if publicity could generate enough business to outpace the associated payroll losses. I recited Proverbs 14:23 to myself, defiantly: "All hard work brings a profit, but mere talk leads only to poverty."

We began fielding calls from clients who feared we would

increase prices in order to afford the $70k policy, even though we had no plans to do so and reassured them we wouldn't increase their rates. Other clients accused Gravity of conducting a communist or socialist experiment that would drive up their own employees' wages and make it more difficult for them to stay in business. One client asked, referring to our customer-support team, "What's their incentive to hustle if you pay them so much?" I wondered when the floodgates would close, if ever.

I could handle the criticism, but the naysayers reminded me of a much more consequential critic—my brother Lucas. When Lucas returned from his travels in 2012 and reengaged as a Gravity board member, he returned to a policy of aggressive financial investment in our team that hadn't been in place when he left. We had just set the goal of 15 percent annual raises, and the company was doing well. In 2013, after observing this policy for close to a year, Lucas asked me out to coffee to discuss the strategic direction of the company. As we sat at Uptown Espresso near the Space Needle in Seattle, it did not take long for him to accuse me of socialist businesses practices. Lucas said he wanted to increase shareholder dividends and for me to buy him out of the company. I could not afford to buy him out, and it didn't make sense to increase dividends when the company was growing so fast and we could be reinvesting our profit back into operations. I told him I would do whatever I could to buy him out as long as it did not jeopardize our employees or the service level we provided to our clients. At the time, he wanted $9 million for his share, a sum that would have devastated the company. I told him I thought he was being unrealistic. We left the coffee shop, tempers flaring.

At this point, there was not much Lucas could do to get his way. Thanks to the deal we had struck in 2008, I had majority control of the company and could outvote him on most types of decisions. So Lucas set out to take me down. As I found out later, he created a list of things he could do to put me in a bad position. On his list were these items: "Negatively affect Dan's reputation; take credit for Gravity Payments' success; make employees question Dan's loyalty; make family question Dan's cruelty; kiss the ring, steal the throne." In early 2014, for the first time ever, Lucas voted against my total compensation for 2013, even though the company had grown over the previous year and I was not seeking a raise.

Lucas's unprecedented actions led me to believe that something was going on behind the scenes. I tried not to let it get to me, though, because I assumed Lucas would come to me with any issues before resorting to legal action. I had no idea the extent to which he was plotting against me. I knew Lucas was in a tough spot and empathized with his position. How would you feel if you thought your kid brother was making decisions that affected your financial situation without your approval? I wanted to find a way to work things out. I wanted to find a way to get him what he wanted. He might not have worked at the company in years, but he had believed in Gravity when there was nothing there to believe in. He deserved a lot for that, but I couldn't figure out how to get him the amount of money he wanted without bankrupting the company.

In late January 2015, I was flying back to Seattle after working with our team in Hawaii when my emotions boiled over on the plane. I had a glass of wine, which went straight to my head. I teared up and wrote to Lucas and his wife, "I regret the fact that we aren't in a position to have an active personal relationship. I do hope for change in that, and I believe both of you do as well. I have spent a lot of time trying to come up with a solution. So far, I don't think I have been able to put the pieces together, but I wanted to at least let you know that I am thinking about each of you and hope you are doing well."

In March 2015, Lucas served me with legal papers saying that if I didn't meet his demands for compensation by buying out his shares or devising some other solution, he would file a lawsuit against me. In response, we came together through lawyers and tried once again to resolve our differences. At the time, Gravity was making about $1.2 million in after-tax profit. We also had about $1.5 million in the bank. In the past, we had invested our profit back into the business to help build new products for our clients, improve customer service, invest in employees, and start new initiatives to grow the company. My brother was now asking for at least $12 million. The interest rate on a loan this large and risky would have been in the double digits, adding significantly to the amount the company would need to repay. Even if we could choke off our practice of investing our profit back into the company, it would still take years to pay off Lucas. To me, it was obvious that this wasn't the right thing to do for

Gravity. The company could not afford it.

We were once again at an impasse. Meanwhile the $70k policy went into effect, and Rush's cries of socialism validated my brother's claims against me. Two weeks after the announcement, Lucas followed through on his threat. He filed suit for breach of contract, breach of fiduciary duty, and minority shareholder oppression. "Since gaining majority control," the complaint read, "Daniel has engaged in a campaign to enrich himself and favor his majority interest in Gravity Payments to the detriment of Lucas and his minority interest." In saying I had overpaid myself (even though we'd mutually agreed upon my salary), deprived him of the increased dividends he wanted, and used company funds for personal enrichment, Lucas claimed I had reneged on the deal we had struck in 2008 when he sold a portion of his shares. He cited the $70k decision as an example of my irresponsible leadership.

I was surprised Lucas had gone forward with the suit. I thought we were going to find a way to work things out, or that he was just bluffing. People threaten lawsuits all the time and never follow through. His resolve made me uneasy. I didn't think his claims were valid, but now that we had a trial date set, my optimism waned. I was in a tight spot. Our profit in 2014 was $2.2 million. I had invested $1.8 million into this new salary program, and now I had to figure out how to pay $100,000 a month in fees for a legal defense against my brother. The math started to become complicated.

I was also worried about the impact the lawsuit could have

on the people at Gravity. If we lost the suit and were required to buy Lucas out for the full value of his shares, we would be forced to sell the entire company. There was no other way to afford it. I owned close to 70 percent of Gravity, so whatever amount Lucas took home in that sale, I would get more than double. Lucas had the company appraised at the end of 2015 and determined that his shares were worth $26 million. If Lucas got his $26 million, I would get more than $50 million. Despite the huge potential payout, I battled against this scenario because I knew the team at Gravity and our clients would suffer as a result. The playbook for acquisitions in our industry reads as follows: lay off all nonessential staff, cut service levels, and raise prices to clients in ways that are difficult to detect. I knew I had to tell our team about the lawsuit and the possibility of this outcome, but I wanted to do more than just inform them. I wanted to make a promise.

We held our summer 2015 quarterly meeting at a brewery near our office. After the regular company updates, I took the stage. I looked out over the group of people who had been by my side through many of the biggest challenges Gravity had faced over the years. I took a deep breath, exhaled, and began to speak. "Shortly after the $70k announcement, I had a lawsuit filed against me." As I watched the faces in the crowd turn solemn, I started speaking more quickly in order to alleviate the uncertainty I had just planted. "I didn't want to make this announcement because it is about my brother, and I really love and care about him," I said after explaining Lucas's claims. "We wouldn't be where we are today without him, so I don't want anyone to come away with a negative viewpoint of him. But I also didn't want anybody to find out about this from anybody other than me."

There was a brief pause. Everyone was staring directly at me. The quiet buzzing at the bar ceased, and even the brewery staff trained their eyes on me. "I have a lot of confidence in us as a team and everything we are doing. So I'm going to make a commitment today: if we lose the lawsuit, I am going to pledge all of my proceeds from the sale of the company, or however much it takes, to ensure that everyone here will be guaranteed their job, as long as they are willing to work, for at least a year."

I thought everyone would be grateful, but everyone just looked concerned. I had miscalculated. Having known about the possibility of a lawsuit for a while, it was hard for me to imagine what it must be like to learn about it for the first time. Everyone was still so stunned by the news that they weren't ready for my solution. They needed time to process the information. Only weeks later did I start receiving encouraging feedback on my plan.

For me, it was important to align my financial incentives with the outcome of the lawsuit. I would no longer get rich if I lost; I would have an obligation to reinvest those funds into our team. That made me proud, and it eased fears in the office. Even if the company failed, I would still be doing what I could to work toward my goal of demonstrating values-driven leadership. We continued forward under the gray cloud of litigation and a growing army of dissenters against our new pay policy. It looked like circumstances would prove all the naysayers, including my brother, correct.

In early August, Patricia Cohen of the *New York Times* published a mostly negative article on the front page of the Sunday Business section. In it she acknowledged the increased awareness we'd received and the new clients we had earned as a result of the new policy, but she tempered that assessment by pointing out that in our business it takes at least a year to actually earn back the cost of bringing new clients onboard. The article also highlighted the employees and clients who had left the company as a result of the new minimum-wage policy. It discussed the lawsuit with my brother and quoted some longtime clients who vehemently disagreed with my decision. In response, several other media outlets ran similar stories. Many of the spin-offs were highly charged versions of the *Times* article, noting the downsides of my plan as well as the lawsuit with Lucas.

In December 2015, *Bloomberg Businessweek* published a devastating profile in which they raised the possibility that the $70k decision was a ploy to distract from Lucas's lawsuit and/or diminish the value of his shares. They also questioned whether my previous seven-figure salary was appropriate for the CEO of a company Gravity's size and whether, as Lucas was alleging, I had decided on the sum against my brother's wishes. The article also referenced some pretty upsetting allegations by my ex-wife Kristie, whom I hadn't seen or spoken to for over two years. I was stunned, but I couldn't blame anyone who read the story for doubting my character and motivations. More than anything I worried about what this meant for Gravity and my ability to share the results of our wage policy.

It had been less than eight months since our original announcement, and the full $70k salary wouldn't take effect for another year. I'd assumed that, if Gravity could remain profitable under our new pay policy, then other business leaders would be forced to pay attention to our example and message. Now that our credibility had been undermined, was I still the best person to deliver this message? Would the shadow of this negative press follow us into the future? Would people care what I had to say if they'd already written me off as a dishonest PR hack?

We'd have to wait to find out.

12
The Trial

WHILE WORK AT GRAVITY consumed most of my time, my new salary forced me to maintain a level of frugality in my personal life that I had not experienced in years. Gone were the days of pushing gray chips to the center of the table and sabering bottles of expensive champagne. To generate extra income, I began renting out my house on Airbnb part-time and stayed with a friend when the house was being rented. My full-time personal assistant, who had been managing my home, cooking meals, and running errands, left to attend medical school, and I stopped searching for someone to replace her. My twelve-year-old car needed several repairs, which I elected to postpone. I had to be extremely careful spending time with other executives because a dinner party that ended with a rogue tab could easily wipe out a week's pay. I continued to downsize my lifestyle.

My trend toward fiscal modesty was not just for me but also for Gravity. The company was in a tough spot. Mounting legal fees and a hiring spree triggered by our increased growth set expenses on an upward trajectory. I am told most people with seven-figure savings prefer to invest their money in a carefully managed and well-diversified portfolio of stocks, mutual funds, and local venture rounds. Not me. I had almost $2 million just sitting in a checking account. It's not that I had no interest in growing my savings; I just wanted to make sure I could use the money at a moment's notice to help Gravity in a cash crunch. Given the increase in the unknowns, I felt the current balance was no longer enough. To increase Gravity's emergency fund, I decided to liquidate some of my material possessions. I mortgaged my $1.3 million home with a view of Puget Sound and took out a loan against my retirement account. Through all of these activities, I was able to increase our safety net to $3 million. I signed all of this money over to Gravity to use in the event the company needed the funds. I had gone from a net worth of $3 million down to zero in a matter of months. I was making less than most of the people who reported directly to me, and I was back to working eighteen-hour days.

For a lot of people, the precariousness of this financial position might send them into panic mode, but I was so focused on the lawsuit, I barely registered the balance in my bank account. I've always been good in a crisis. Instead of letting my emotions get the better of me, I turn stoic, tuning out anything that isn't vital in order to focus on the task at hand. Rather than let myself grieve the loss of my relationship with Lucas or allow the fear of losing Gravity get the better of me, I put all my energy into getting through the trial as best I could. I started replaying the past over and over in my head. I tried to recall conversations and interactions I'd had years prior in order to figure out whether Lucas's lawyers could use them as a case against me. I reviewed thousands of old emails and tried to see them through the judge's eyes. This exercise of self-investigation was exhausting, but I hoped it would prepare me for my day in court.

I n his book *The Art of Happiness,* the Dalai Lama explains how unrealistically high expectations make you unhappy. In the context of the lawsuit, my brother had set his expectations at $26 million by the spring of 2016. It didn't take a genius to look at our situation and say, "Why don't these two brothers just settle? They could both get exactly what they want. Lucas could get a multimillion-dollar payout, Dan could get full control of the company, and they could both then get to work repairing their relationship." At this point, we were apparently the only two humans on earth who thought we couldn't (or shouldn't) just sit down and work it out. I couldn't figure out why that was. Fraternal rivalry? Greed? Hubris? I racked my brain for a solution but found nothing. We tried several times to settle the suit outside of court, but to no avail. In June 2016, more than a year after the $70k wage policy took effect, the trial began.

The courtroom was definitely not like those in TV shows. In place of elegant windows and dramatic ambiance were off-white walls and oppressive lighting. Scuffs on the linoleum floor were evidence of the many battles fought in that room. A dozen

Gravity team members filled the dark wooden benches, which reminded me of the pews in our church back in Idaho. Several journalists also attended, guaranteeing every word uttered in the trial would be broadcast not only to the judge but also to the public at large.

"All rise!" the bailiff called. Everyone in the room stood awkwardly. Judge Theresa Doyle walked out of her chambers in the customary black robe. She was a petite, stylish woman, and her expression signaled she was not going to take any crap. "Please be seated," she said.

I looked over at my brother, surrounded by his attorneys and paralegals. Lucas had been one of my closest friends. Despite our many disagreements while trying to get Gravity off the ground, we had been inseparable. We traveled together; we talked every single day. In 2006, when he went on his first date with his now wife, Shannon, he had called me right afterward because he wanted me to know first. I once again wondered how we had strayed so far from those days.

"This is an unfortunate tale of ego, anger, and resentment from Dan Price and his unwillingness to live with the deal that he agreed to in 2008." Thus began the opening arguments from my brother's attorney. In the process of discovery, we had turned over more than half a million pages of emails, notes, text messages, instant messages, tweets, comments, LinkedIn messages, Facebook messages, speech transcripts, documents, and financial data on Gravity. My brother had picked out the twenty or thirty documents that portrayed me in the worst light, and his attorneys started calling them out one by one. They were up on the projector to paint me as an overpaid CEO who used the company as his own personal piggy bank. They presented old company credit card statements and asked me to remember the business purpose behind meals I'd eaten and paid for six years ago. They presented several of my emails with accountants and consultants, asking me to explain why I had used this verb or that adjective, in an attempt to prove that I was engaging in backroom dealings. They asked me a half-dozen times about my relationship with the supermodel Tyra Banks, who had become a close friend and confidante. It was intimidating to have to maintain focus while highly experienced attorneys tried to solicit some sort of misleading admission from me, but I somehow managed to get through the examination without losing my composure. I reminded myself that all of these events had transpired over the last decade. This was the greatest hits of my least-admirable behavior compressed into several hours of testimony. The examples presented also had little to do with the legal issues at hand. This lack of connection to the law made me realize that this trial wasn't about money or shareholder oppression; it was an emotional battle between two brothers. It was a battle for recognition of our respective roles in the success of Gravity.

After Lucas's two-day testimony early in the trial, I sent an email to him. "I appreciated you sharing so many things over the last two court days," I wrote. "I also appreciate the fact that I needed to just sit there and be quiet and listen." I told him it was good for me to hear his side of the story in such detail. I told him I was sad about the circumstances but recognized part of the reason we were sitting in court was the result of the success we had created together. "This dispute sucks, but some of it comes from some of our successes, and of course some of it comes from some of our failures. I want to share that I can recognize the successes also."

He didn't reply, but his wife did. She attended every day of the trial, sitting in the back taking notes and smiling. "Thanks for your email," she said. "I appreciate it." After that, she and I started chatting during the breaks in the trial. We greeted each other in the morning and said goodbye when court adjourned. Although the circumstances leading up to the situation were awful, I was happy to be in the same room as my brother and his wife. We hadn't seen each other or spoken in some time, and the proceedings truly felt like a formal way for us to work out our differences and communicate. Maybe, I thought, this would allow us to finally heal our rift and move past the challenges of the past few years.

The trial lasted three weeks. Closing arguments proceeded much as the opening statements had. In a final display of theatrics, my brother's attorney poured red-dyed water into clear water to symbolize my alleged blending of business and personal expenses. My attorney, Paul, closed with a straightforward but dry recitation of facts and legal issues. The difference between the slick, hotshot performance from Lucas's Harvard Law attorney versus our careful, modest presentation made me nervous. The trial sputtered to completion, coming back to life only when the judge finally spoke. She acknowledged the unique nature of our relationship as brothers and then told everyone that she would have a decision ready in three weeks.

Many friends and acquaintances reached out to me after the trial. I was expecting people to tell me there was too much risk outstanding and that I should find a way to come up with the money to buy Lucas out before the judge ruled. No one did. They told me I was in a good position and should just wait for the judge's decision. I am always skeptical when all of the advice is similar. I wonder: "What are they missing? What am I missing?" I knew there was a solution. I just hadn't found it yet.

I began to have terrifyingly clear visions of the judge's mandate. In my imagination, she kept saying, "I'm ordering a buyout of Lucas Price's shares at twenty-six million dollars. I'm ordering that you pay three million dollars in damages. I'm further ordering that you pay one million dollars in legal fees." Then I imagined myself walking over to Lucas, shaking his hand, and shaking his attorneys' hands.

These visions were made clearer by the inherent uncertainty of the legal system. I knew the judge was an expert in the law. She had asked intelligent questions and had demonstrated a thorough understanding of the issues at play. But judges don't specialize in the type of cases they hear. They try everything from divorces to murders, and her lack of business specialization made me worry. I knew the worst-case scenario could actually come to pass.

Before she announced her decision, the judge decided to email it out instead of reading it in court. Without an in-person decision, I would never get the chance to shake Lucas's hand. I wanted to be back in the room with him so we could talk. What if I never got the opportunity to reconcile with him? That thought pained me most of all.

The night before the judge was due to issue her decision, I decided to go play poker with several friends, all of whom were experienced leaders, to take my mind off the situation. But I couldn't concentrate on the game. All I could think about was the lawsuit. I started rambling. "Look: The highest I've offered Lucas is fourteen million dollars. The lowest Lucas has offered is eighteen million. The gap isn't so big. I have to find a way to bridge the gap." A few of the guys around the table looked back at me in annoyance. I could tell they weren't excited to be talking shop at the poker table, but I was so caught up in my own emotions that I couldn't stop. "The gap is only four million dollars, but the problem is I haven't even figured out how I can come up with the first fourteen million. So it's not as if I have to come up with four million. It's that I have to come up with eighteen."

"Dan. You're freaking out," my friend Ryan said. "Just relax. Stay calm. Don't think about it, because there's really nothing you can do about it at this point." His advice did absolutely no good. I couldn't even look at my cards.

"You playin', or are you just gonna sit there?" Ryan asked when I forgot to check. He looked annoyed. "Man, you're so self-absorbed. You can't stop talking about your situation." I couldn't decide if he was being sarcastic.

"Sorry guys. I have to go." I dropped my cards and put down a few bills to buy my way out of the game early. No one said anything. I stood and walked out of the house onto the street. The late-evening sun that graces Seattle in July was long gone. I thought about heading home, but I knew the house was empty. I needed to talk to somebody. Standing outside of my car on a hill overlooking the Seattle skyline, I scrolled through the contacts in my phone. I stopped on the name of one of my closest friends. He and I had been through many late-night conversations when his company was running short of money and in need of a solution. I clicked on his name. After several rings, there was no answer. I dialed again. I figured he would know it was important if I called twice.

"Hey, Dan." He sounded preoccupied. "I just landed at the airport. What's up?"

"I need to talk to somebody. I have twelve hours before the judge issues her decision."

"Well, I had a really early morning, and I had a late flight. Can we just talk tomorrow?"

"Tomorrow is too late."

"Yeah, I'm just not really free right now."

"Dude, I really need to talk to you."

"Okay, well, let me go home, see how I feel, and I'll call you."

"Okay, fine." I hung up, got in my car, and headed home.

Back at the house, I was greeted by Mikey, my dog. I dropped some food in Mikey's bowl and waited for the call. My phone sat on the table, silent.

When it became obvious that my friend wasn't going to call me back, I decided to try a new tactic. I sat down at my computer, pulled up various online financial calculators, and scanned every blog I could find that would help shed light on my situation. I didn't know exactly what I was looking for but thought there was a chance I would come across some helpful bit of information. Finally, I closed the screen and rested my elbows on the desk in my bedroom. I looked out over Elliott Bay. Lights from downtown Seattle illuminated a large swath of water near the shore. I pulled up my phone again. The screen showed no new activity. I sent a text message to Paul, my attorney. "Are you up?" I received a reply within seconds.

"Yeah, what's up?"

"I really need to talk. Can I call you?" No reply. Even the guy who could make an easy $200 on a twenty-five-minute call wouldn't speak to me. I climbed into bed, pulled out my computer once again, and drifted off to sleep while responding to emails.

The next morning, I was up before six o'clock. I called Paul. "Let's find a way."

"All right, I'll call Lucas's lawyer and let him know to expect a proposal."

I came up with a proposal whereby I would pay my brother $10 million if I won the suit and $19 million if I lost the suit. To me, this closed down the extremes, giving us both some peace of mind. The judge would still be involved, but she would have less latitude. I proposed this idea to my lawyer, who passed it to my brother. I could tell the idea was getting traction when I received a counteroffer. We parried and postured, closing in on a settlement. Proposals started coming in with greater frequency. It was clear there was mutual motivation to make this new path work.

At noon, we were discussing terms, interest rates, and security around the payments. Some of the items proposed brought us closer to agreement. Other items took us further apart, and we had to claw back with concessions and alterations. I agreed to increase the upper end of the buyout price if my brother prevailed. In exchange, I proposed reducing the lower end if I prevailed. I hated this horse-trading style of negotiation. I have never been comfortable in these situations. They lack creativity and usually fail to produce anything more than a zero-sum outcome. With every change in terms, only one side can win.

At 3:30 p.m. Lucas rejected my latest proposal through his lawyer. I was surprised; I had thought we were making progress. My brother seemed so sure of himself. He didn't even put forth a new proposal. His confidence that he could get to the number he wanted diminished my already negative appraisal of my situation.

I weighed my options. Time was clearly running out. What I did in these next few minutes could define the rest of my life. I could lose Gravity Payments with a single stroke of the judge's pen. Inspired by this extreme risk, I began to formulate another proposal, further conceding on terms and price. I had spent months trying to put myself in my brother's shoes, attempting to figure out what was going on in his head and how he must be feeling. This agonizing empathy, coupled with my often-extreme paranoia, convinced me I would lose the suit. I knew I had a strong legal argument, but emotionally I wouldn't allow myself to consider any outcome other than defeat. As I started to type out another proposal, my mind battled my heart. The phone rang. It was Paul.

For several minutes, we discussed the proposal I was trying to formulate. We discussed ways we could add to it, ways to make it better for Lucas. We went back and forth on a few issues. All of a sudden, Paul went silent. When he finally spoke, his voice was faint. "She just ruled," he muttered.

"What?" I replied immediately.

"I just got an email."

"What does it say?"

"I haven't read it. I'll send it over." The email crept its way through the fiber cables. Finally, it popped up in my inbox. I struggled to download it.

"Just read it to me," I cried in desperation. I was losing control of my emotions. I was on the verge of tears. "Just tell me what she said!" Silence. "You don't have to read it first. Just read it to me now!" Against my instructions, I knew he was reading it. I was struck with an unusual bolt of intense anger. "Just read it to me!"

"Holy cow! Dan, oh my gosh!" My heart sank. A million thoughts raced through my head. I thought of losing my life's work. I thought of having to face everyone at Gravity. The voice on the other end finally curtailed my delirious downward spiral. "Okay, Dan. I'm looking through this. It's a long document. It's thirty-two pages long, so I really don't want to tell you what it says because I'm afraid I might have missed something. I'm only reading the bottom, but I'm going to read it to you." There was another painful pause. "'Based on the foregoing findings of fact and conclusions of law, it is now ordered, adjudged, and decreed that Lucas Price has failed to prove his claims in this matter. Judgment shall be entered in favor of Dan Price. Dan Price is entitled to an award of his reasonable attorneys' and paralegals' fees and expenses of litigation incurred in defense of this action.' I'm looking for something else, but it looks like she ruled for you on everything. Everything. Attorneys' fees and all."

I started bawling. A wave of sadness swept over me. I was sad for Lucas and sad about the whole situation. I wailed on the phone. I was completely alone at my house, sitting on the couch in my living room. Finally, I composed myself enough to say, "Paul, I wish I could give you a hug right now." Another pause, and then he replied. "Hey, Dan, let's talk another time."

I heard a beep as he hung up the phone.

13
Gifts

THE CFO SAYS TO THE CEO, "Boss, I've been looking at the numbers, and I don't think we can afford to invest in the development of our employees. I'm worried about what will happen if we invest a ton of money in them and then they leave."

The CEO thinks about this statement for a moment and then replies. "But what if we don't invest in them, and they stay?"

My dad first told me this corporate parable many years ago, but the true meaning didn't sink in until several months after we announced the $70k policy. When you're a disinterested third party observing the situation, the absurdity of the CFO's position is clear. In practice, when you are a CEO down in the trenches, fighting with your own money, you can easily find yourself on the wrong side of this decision without realizing it. Only later do you look back and realize your mistake. It's easy to say you think each member of your team is an asset when in fact you really look at them as an expense.

The CEO's position in this story is no doubt risky. At Gravity, we have taken losses by investing in certain members of our team who didn't stay with us or who weren't right for the job, but that's no reason to change philosophies. Overall, I have seen the benefits of aggressive investment far outweigh the downsides. As a result, I am always looking for ways I can do a better job of investing in our team. The best part about this strategy is when I am rewarded with the unexpected.

Now that the lawsuit was over and implementation of the $70k policy was underway, I started wondering how I could up the ante even more. Before I could propose anything else, however, the team at Gravity turned the tables on me.

Behind my back, a technical support representative at Gravity named Alyssa O'Neal was hatching a plan. A single mother who had been living far from the office in a relatively inexpensive part of the city, Alyssa was greatly affected by the $70k policy. She was able to move into a bigger house closer to the office. She was able to take her five-year-old son, Jaice, to Disneyland for the first time and provide a better life for him. She was frustrated with the way I was being portrayed in the media. She was fed up with the disparity between the man I was being made out to be and the man she worked with every day. So, she decided to take matters into her own hands.

In July 2016, just over a year after the wage announcement and a few days after the judge ruled in my favor against Lucas, we were scheduled to hold one of our quarterly meetings. Several days before, I was presented with a meeting agenda that seemed fairly typical. The meeting was scheduled for late in the afternoon. I had spent so many of these pre-meeting mornings agonizing over big announcements such as the $70k decision or Lucas filing his lawsuit, and I was relieved to finally have what I thought would be a straightforward meeting.

I sat in the front row and watched as our newly hired team members were introduced. Partway through the meeting, Daniel, our company comedian and perennial meeting emcee, asked me to stand up and say a few words. In the five seconds it took me to get to my feet and walk to the microphone, I devised a speech focused on encouraging everyone to challenge themselves and to keep up their hard work. As I started to speak, I scanned the faces in the crowd. I looked to the back of the room, and my eyes settled on someone unexpected. "Stephan?" I said, pausing my speech. "What are you doing here?"

I had met Stephan Aarstol, CEO of the California-based company Tower Paddle Boards, almost a year earlier, after he had reached out to me. He had been inspired by the $70k decision, but instead of raising his team's salaries, he took a different path toward employee well-being. Realizing that his people would likely be more satisfied at work if they were fulfilled in their personal lives, he reduced his company's workday to five hours instead of the standard eight-plus.

I was dumbfounded. He'd made the trip from California without telling me about it? Stephan just smiled as the shock registered on my face. "It's a surprise!" someone shouted. "Keep going." I resumed my speech, wondering what was happening. I hate surprises because I like to feel in control and aware of what's going on. In this instance, however, I realized the best way to get more information was just to be patient. I wrapped up my impromptu spiel and sat back down.

As the meeting neared its close, Phil, a member of our sales team, came up and stood in front of the microphone. "I have a confession to make," he started. "It says on the agenda I'm going to talk about the new Gravity T-shirts . . . I'm not going to talk about that." He proceeded to introduce Stephan, who walked to the front of the room and began to speak.

"I'm here to show my appreciation to Dan and the whole Gravity team," Stephan began. "You've changed the lives of my employees and made a huge positive impact on our company." He went on to mention how back in early 2015, before he had implemented the shorter-workday policy, a business magazine had asked him to write an article about all the benefits of a five-hour workday. "I found I could hire all these young employees right out of college for not very much and I could work them really hard. I didn't want to give that up. But then on April 13, 2015, when Dan shook the business world with this idea for the seventy-thousand-dollar minimum wage, I said to myself, 'This is insane. He's not just talking. He did something.' Four days later, my five-hour workday article published. Because of Dan, I asked myself, 'Why am I just talking about this? Why can't I do something?'"

I jumped up and gave Stephan a big hug. I felt as if a big secret had been leaked and was now being whispered throughout the corporate world. Stephan and I both understood that the old way of treating employees, as an expense to be minimized, just wasn't as effective as treating them as valuable assets and human beings. It hindered growth and kept everyone from realizing their full potential. Research by Zeynep Ton, Raj Sisodia, Shawn Achor, Daniel Pink, Daniel Kahneman, and many others had highlighted this concept, but we were actually living it. Stephan's words made me realize the new way of doing business wasn't about a $15-per-hour minimum wage (which had just been passed by the city of Seattle) or a $70,000-per-year minimum wage imposed by a CEO. It was a new mentality. It was a shift in thinking from "How can I reduce expenses more today?" to "How can I invest more in my team today?" Whether it was giving people more time or more money or something else, I knew in that moment that this movement would prevail. I couldn't stop smiling.

Listening to Stephan's speech, I also realized that while plenty of businesspeople, writers, advocates, etc., had been talking about the benefits of increased wages and reduced working hours—among other initiatives—talking about them and actually putting them into practice are two very different things. The old ways are so entrenched, the profit-driven mentality so pervasive, that going against the grain requires not only a shift in perspective but also a healthy appetite for risk and ridicule. I'd made my decision after years of debating with myself about what my duty as an entrepreneur entailed. While I'd certainly had grand visions of changing the business landscape as we know it and serving as a positive example to others who were considering similar moves, ultimately my decision had been selfish. I was trying to prove something to myself, to show that I could live a life aligned with the values I had always said were most dear to me. I knew that I had a responsibility to myself and to my company to run Gravity in a way I believed was right. *Not* instituting a $70k minimum wage when I knew deep down that it was the right thing to do would have been the real failure. You can't be a leader and only follow the status quo. You have to think for yourself. You have to be your own CEO.

After Stephan spoke, I assumed the surprise was over and the meeting was coming to a close, but instead Phillip returned to the stage. He presented me with a book containing portraits of Gravity employees along with notes they had written to me. Several people read excerpts. "Prior to Gravity, I spent virtually my entire career working in the nonprofit sector because I thought I wouldn't be able to find for-profit work that aligned with my values . . . I was wrong." "I feel blessed to have found a company that holds true to my values and strives to make a difference each day." As I listened, I could feel my emotions strengthen. I smiled, but mostly in an effort to fight back tears.

Alyssa read last. "You've been a great leader and an inspiration throughout my time here at Gravity," she began. "I'm thankful for all the opportunities you've given us. I honestly don't know where I would be if it weren't for Gravity." Alyssa went on to explain how her life had changed since the $70k policy went into effect. She finished to applause. I reached for the book, but Alyssa held it back from me. "I'm actually going to hold on to this," she said. "Because we have one more surprise for you."

"Okay," I replied. I had no idea what to expect. Alyssa had a sheepish smile that suggested she was harboring a combination of nervousness, guilt, and excitement.

"But," Alyssa started, "it's outside." A million thoughts went through my head, but I didn't have time to come to any conclusions. As we walked out of the room, everyone stood up and followed us down the hall. Alyssa led this great procession of those I saw, in a sense, as my family. My head spun. We reached the parking lot and there, ten yards away, was a brand-new blue Tesla Model S with a huge green bow on the roof. The license plate was fitted with a custom Gravity Payments backing. Immediately, my smile broke. I burst into tears.

Over the years, I had made comments on social media and in person about how much I loved the idea of owning a Tesla. I liked the fact that Tesla was trying to take down the established automobile industry, especially the archaic and miserable car-sales model. For me, it was the ultimate vehicle. I am constantly battling my excitement over expensive luxuries in the interest of using my money toward more worthwhile pursuits. For years, I had warded off the desire to purchase a Tesla even though I could have afforded it.

Alyssa knew this and decided to get it for me. She wrapped her arms around me and also began to cry. I didn't know what to think, and I didn't know what to do. I wanted to ask so many questions. I wanted to know how the team had made this happen. Most of all, I was overcome with emotions I had never experienced. It was as if the feelings I had contained for the previous eighteen months were all being released in that moment. All of the amazing memories, the challenges, the victories, and the stories rushed to the surface.

Finally, I was able to utter the words, "Thank you." Everyone started to clap. Someone popped the front trunk. Inside was a plaque the team had signed. It read:

> *Thank you for always putting the team before yourself.*
>
> *This gift is our way of showing how much your sacrifice means to us.*

I still didn't know what to do. Someone encouraged me to open the rear trunk. When I finally figured out how to open it, two of our remote team members, Brad and Garret, who had decided to drive eight hours each way to be part of the surprise, piled out. They had been hiding inside for the last several minutes.

"How did you do this?" I yelled. "How did you do this?" Everyone just kept smiling. Apparently, they were all committed to silence.

"Just enjoy it!" someone yelled back.

I later found out how they pulled it off. Alyssa and her team discovered that it wouldn't be that expensive, per person, to make payments on a car if a lot of people were contributing. They knew the car was something I had wanted for a long time but would never buy for myself; it was the ultimate gift. So, they went to work figuring out exactly how to surprise me with the car of my dreams.

It took months. The team negotiated with Tesla, and they debated amongst themselves. They held all-company meetings without my knowledge. Later I learned they had questioned whether the car was too flashy and whether I would feel guilty driving it. Finally, an uneasy consensus was reached to move forward with the purchase. As the plans fell into place over the next few months, support became stronger and stronger.

The morning of the quarterly meeting, Alyssa and three other members of the Gravity team went down to the dealership, signed for the car, and drove it very carefully out of the lot. They pulled it into a parking garage across the street from our office and allowed other members of the team to go out and take peeks throughout the day. The plaque was affixed, and right before Alyssa led me out to the parking lot, Brad and Garret had hopped into the trunk for the surprise.

I will forever remember that day as one of the happiest of my life. My happiness really had nothing to do with the car, though. For me, it was about how much we had disrupted the status quo of business. We had come a long way from paying employees $24,000 a year. Money no longer played as prominent a role in our daily routine. We were focused on what truly mattered. As we mingled in the parking lot, cracked a few beers, and talked amongst ourselves, I looked around and realized how young I really was. I realized how much time we all had left to make a difference. I couldn't wait to find out what more this team could accomplish.

14
Rewards

AS I WRITE THIS BOOK, almost four years after I announced the new minimum wage, I am still reading new critiques of our policy on political and business blogs. It is painful to be on the receiving end of such jabs, but I have begun to see the upside to the criticism. The backlash tells me we are onto something. It tells me this new way of doing business will actually work. If it couldn't work, there would be no need for the pundits to take notice and try to sow doubt. The fact that Gravity is supposedly upending the traditional economic model terrifies those who have spent lifetimes clinging to a self-serving illusion of the perfect market theory. The more success we see, the more destructive I expect the opposition to become.

A year after the $70k announcement, I took some time to reflect on the results. It was clear the decision had been a success from a financial perspective, but more important, it was a dream come true for us as a team and me as a leader. Our profit had doubled, our revenue growth had doubled, our clients and employees were both staying with us longer. The year before the announcement, we generated $15 million in revenue. Less than four years later, as this book goes to print, we are on pace for $50 million next year. As Harvard Business School professor Michael Wheeler stated on a *PBS NewsHour* special on Gravity in late 2016, "On balance, it's prospered."

I also had our team take a closer look at how the raises had actually affected individuals who worked at the company. The results were surprising. The fifty employees who received raises started moving closer to the office. Their combined commute time shrank by many hours each week. Not only has decreased commute time been linked to increased happiness and well-being—a fact to which some Gravity employees can certainly attest—but all that extra time could now be dedicated to activities far more important than driving.

We've also seen an increase in retirement savings. The individuals affected by the raise increased their annual voluntary 401(k) contributions by an average of 130 percent. As with the reduced commute times, with a reduction in the anxiety inherent in building a retirement nest egg, the people at Gravity can now turn their attention toward more fulfilling activities.

One of those fulfilling activities was starting a family. In previous years, we had no more than two new-baby announcements each year. In the year after the $70k announcement, ten Gravity team members—many of them first-time parents—had a baby or announced they were having one. It was our own personal baby boom. We were all working hard, but our lives were improving. The greatest success of our $70k policy, and the thing that made it most worth it, is that more than forty babies have joined our Gravity family since our announcement.

Employee satisfaction also moved along an interesting path. As I've explained, I made the $70k decision in an effort to reduce our team's financial distractions, not because I thought a higher salary would make them happier. Pay alone does not equal happiness, and I can prove it. Every week, we use an online survey system called TINYpulse to ask our employees a single anonymous question about working at Gravity. Although we rotate questions every week, we do have one recurring question that comes up once per month: "On a scale of 1 to 10, how happy are you at work?" Since research has shown that people are not very good at evaluating their own happiness, a question like this really just measures their curent level of satisfaction, not their actual well-being. Prior to the $70k announcement, our average score remained steady for months at about 8 out of 10. According to TINYpulse, this is pretty much as high as it goes for most companies; they say you're chasing your tail if you try to go any higher than that. I always want to be better, but I didn't prioritize an effort to push this number higher.

After the $70k announcement, the next survey asking the satisfaction question came back with an average of 9 out of 10. The following month, we were down to 8.6. The month after that, it was 8.3. Since then, we have hovered between 7.5 and 8. It took exactly three months for the people who work at Gravity to acclimate to their new situation. This phenomenon, known as "hedonic adaptation" or the "hedonic treadmill" is well documented in psychology, including by Daniel Kahneman who coauthored the salary and well-being study that had inspired our $70k decision. Basically, because happiness or joy is a more transient emotion than general well-being, humans tend to become less happy over time when the novelty of a new situation or experience wears off. By contrast, changes in well-being, which is measured by one's general satisfaction with their life, often produce much more long-term effects.

Although we didn't have a baseline to measure the change in actual well-being of our team before and after the decision, I suspect this metric would have been less fickle. Our team was making meaningful adjustments to their lives—reducing commutes, saving money, starting families—that have been shown to increase well-being. Lives were improving, but we weren't creating some type of corporate utopia where everyone suddenly stopped gunning for higher pay, a bigger house, or a better job title. Although those things don't bring us true, lasting happiness, we are human and will always have them on our minds to some degree.

As the Bible says in 1 Timothy 6:10, the love of money is the root of all evil. Money isn't inherently evil, but the obsession with it is. And that obsession can take many forms. While lack of money was a distraction for lower earners, money was equally distracting for me when I began to use it as a scorecard for success. Every time money is pushed to the forefront of our minds, it crushes creativity, creates pain, and erodes our lives. It's best left alone, out of sight and out of mind. We were witnessing firsthand the benefits of fine-tuning money out of our lives.

Many commentators have felt the need to speculate on my motivations in raising Gravity's minimum wage: Perhaps it's narcissism. Perhaps it's a desire to be a hero or prove others wrong. I can understand why people might think these things but even if you doubt my motivations, the positive impact of the policy is undeniable. Our success and the dissemination of the $70k story did not just impact Gravity. As Patricia Cohen of the *New York Times* wrote in July 2015, "There are times when Dan Price feels as if he stumbled into the middle of the street with a flag and found himself at the head of a parade." That's a fair metaphor; at times, I have certainly felt that I've become the poster boy for this idea.

In an article one year after the $70k announcement, *USA Today* wrote of our policy, "The swashbuckling move struck a national nerve." Professor Ryan Buell of Harvard Business School began teaching a case study on Gravity conducted by several of his colleagues, including Michael Norton and Mitchell Weiss. Not only did Buell say that the case study made his students more uncomfortable, more engaged, and more divided than any other topic, he also told us that "an increase in the minimum wage is gaining momentum, both through public policy and through company-by-company decisions. One of the first snowballs that started this avalanche was Dan's announcement."

Many independent business owners and CEOs have reached out to me, wanting to discuss changes at their companies. One note came in from Tony Tran, owner of Third and Loom, which runs factories in Vietnam. He worked with me to come up with the Vietnamese equivalent to $70,000 and implemented this as the minimum wage at his company, doubling his workers' previous average pay. Mario Zahariev, owner of Gravity client Pop's Pizza & Pasta in the Seattle area, decided to take the expected savings of using us as his credit card processor and invest it right back into employee salaries. CEO Megan Driscoll of Boston-based Pharmalogics raised the base salary of her recruiting staff by 33 percent, to $50,000. Since the recruiters were partially paid on commission, this increased base salary provided more financial stability. One note that captures the essence of this movement came from a CEO who wrote that she simply could not afford to give anyone on her team one extra dollar. Despite her financial situation, she said she planned to work as hard as she could to be able to invest in her team in the future.

It wasn't just small companies that were making waves. Many big companies made similar moves in the years directly following the $70k announcement. In July 2016, Starbucks increased the wages of its lowest-paid workers by between 5 and 15 percent. That same month, J. P. Morgan Chase increased the salaries of its lowest-paid workers by between 20 and 60 percent in a multiyear, scaled plan. Weeks later, REI announced a similar move. Later that year, the *New York Times* reported that Walmart, which had implemented a $10-an-hour minimum wage in early 2015, was experiencing increased sales at a time when overall sales in the general merchandise-retailing industry were down. Customer-service scores had improved consistently, and employees were spending more at Walmart's locations. "In the short term, the Walmart experiment shows pretty clearly that paying people better improves both the work force and the shoppers' experience," the *Times* reported. In discussing Walmart's success, the *Times* posed the same question I had asked myself when originally deciding to increase wages at Gravity: "What if paying workers more, training them better, and offering better opportunities for advancement can actually make a company more profitable, rather than less?"

Three years after implementing the $10-an-hour minimum wage, Walmart again increased its hourly wage, this time to $11. Later that year, the world's second trillion-dollar company (and Walmart's largest competitor), Amazon, announced it would start paying $15 an hour to all of its American employees. According to the company, the move would increase the hourly wages of more than 350,000 full-time, part-time, and seasonal workers. One could argue that neither move is as generous as the companies make them out to be: Walmart, for instance, announced it was closing dozens of its Sam's Club stores the same day it announced the new wage hike. Amazon scrapped a popular employee bonus and preferred-stock program in order to "afford" the new hourly rate. Many argued that Amazon's move was designed to make it more competitive—just in time for the holiday season—in a tightening labor market. And when one considers that several of the states where both Amazon and Walmart have workers are already on track to increase wages—to $12 an hour or higher—in the next few years, the impact of these new minimums becomes much less impressive.

Regardless of their motivations, the fact that America's two largest employers have decided to pay their people more makes me optimistic for the future of our economy and society. Even if Walmart and Amazon are acting out of self-interest or succumbing to pressure, the fact that this pressure exists should be a reason for optimism. Companies and states are increasing their minimum wages thanks to monumental pressure from people who have seen the cracks in our capitalist facade. While many still use the term "socialist" as an epithet, more and more people are beginning to demand greater accountability and fairer treatment from the private sector. They believe that businesses have a responsibility to our society and should not be solely focused on making as much money as possible. According to an annual survey by Deloitte, even though 83 percent of millennials—of which I am one—believe that a business's success should be measured by more than just financial performance, 67 percent of them believe that businesses have no ambition beyond making money. As this generation continues to have more power and influence over business—as employees, consumers, and leaders—they will continue to put pressure on the system to bend to their will. [5]

This new revolution is just in its infancy, but it is spreading quickly. As more momentum builds, this shift will be harder and harder to reverse. By setting in motion this positive feedback loop, we will not only turn business into an unstoppable force for good, we will create a better world for generations to come.

---

5. Deloitte Insights, "2018 Deloitte Millennial Survey: Millennials disappointed in business, unprepared for Industry 4.0," ed. Matthew Budman and Abrar Khan, 2018, https://www2.deloitte.com/content/dam/Deloitte/global/Documents/About-Deloitte/gx-2018-millennial-survey-report.pdf.

15
A New Test

IN EARLY 2017, I was given the chance to show the world that Gravity's success was not a fluke created by media exposure. The story starts in December 2013, when, out of the blue, I received a call from a man named Phil Telesco. In 2004, Phil and his business partners had founded ChargeItPro, an integrated payments company based in San Francisco. ChargeItPro works with software providers that cater to small businesses, enabling them to seamlessly accept credit card payments from within their point-of-sale systems. Like Gravity, the company is dedicated to helping independent businesses compete with their much larger competitors.

Phil had first heard about Gravity several years prior, when we were still in our infancy, and had been intrigued by our business model and rapid growth. In 2011, he relocated his company to Boise, not far from where I'd grown up, and was reminded of Gravity when his sister Stephanie (owner of the legendary Boise eatery Brick Oven Bistro) sent him an article about us from the *Idaho Press-Tribune.* On our call, Phil told me he'd saved the article and had been meaning to reach out because he thought our values were aligned and we might be able to work together in some capacity.

Later, I would learn that Phil had also reached out to us because he was thinking about a succession plan for his company. ChargeItPro was growing rapidly, but Phil knew he wouldn't be able to lead it forever and wanted to explore his options long before he was forced to sell. Having previously sold another business to a large company in a deal that did not end well, Phil knew that acquisitions often end badly for employees, and he was committed to doing what he could to avoid that fate for his workers. Phil saw ChargeItPro less as a company and more as a family. If he left, he wanted to leave his team with a partner who cared about his employees' futures and well-being, someone who wouldn't resort to layoffs or other schemes to financially engineer the company. Having heard about our culture, he thought Gravity might be a good candidate, but he wanted to be sure.

Phil and I met several times over the next few months and began to explore ways in which we might work together. In early 2014, we worked out a deal whereby ChargeItPro would switch its primary vendor relationship and Gravity would take over as its processor. The deal was a win-win, as Gravity got a great new partner and ChargeItPro benefited from the improved levels of service our team was able to provide over the larger processors. Phil had always prided himself on putting his customers first and going above and beyond to serve their needs, even if it meant he had to answer support calls himself. In his interactions with our team, Phil saw that we shared that same dedication to helping our clients succeed. As time went on, he grew more and more confident in our partnership.

As the months went on, our conversations eventually turned to the prospect of Phil selling ChargeItPro to Gravity. After working together for almost three years, we settled on a deal in which Gravity would purchase ChargeItPro and I would become CEO. ChargeItPro would become a fully owned subsidiary, meaning all fifty of its employees would be my responsibility.

I was excited at the prospect of bringing on this great new partner and growing Gravity in the process, but I also foresaw several complications. For instance, although we share a lot of the same values, Phil took an old-school, top-down approach to management, and I worried how his team would adapt to Gravity's culture of autonomy and "be your own CEO" attitude. I had no intention of laying people off to save money, but what if Phil's people weren't the right fit for our team?

Additionally, there was the question of employee salaries. Most of ChargeItPro's technical-support team members were earning $28,000 per year. I didn't know any of them at the time, but I knew I couldn't lead a company that was paying so little. I knew if Gravity purchased ChargeItPro, we would have to raise the salaries of the lowest-paid team members. It made the financial prospects for the deal much worse for Gravity, but Phil recognized this. He wanted his team to find a good home, so he discounted the purchase price to account for a portion of the salary increases. While most people try to get the best financial outcome for themselves in such a sale, Phil put the welfare of his team ahead of his own windfall. With little fanfare, we closed the deal in March 2017.

As soon as the acquisition closed, however, the outlook at Gravity began to evolve. As I prepared to increase the minimum salary at ChargeItPro, many of my top executives advised caution. Unlike the situation when I announced the $70k policy at Gravity, I didn't have a sizable personal financial buffer to bail out the company. Most of my money was already in use inside the company. I had two mortgages on my house. We had just spent more than a million dollars building out our new headquarters in Seattle, having finally outgrown our old space for good. Most important, we had borrowed $12 million—three times Gravity's expected annual profit—to buy ChargeItPro. We were in debt, with no backstop.

Friends and peers acknowledged my tough position. If I didn't raise the new group's salaries, my actions would not only contradict my words, they would also fly in the face of my goal to change the way business is done. If I raised their salaries and we defaulted on the loan, I would be my critics' case study of failure. Everyone at Gravity and ChargeItPro would be looking for new jobs.

Searching for answers, I met my dad for coffee one day in Boise. He told me I had to raise the wages. He wasn't sure it was the objectively correct business decision, but because of what I had done and said in the past, it was the only way to operate with integrity. "You're trapped. I don't think you have much choice," he said. "The reality is you gotta figure out a way to make it work." He then qualified his statement. "This is still a business, and you have to have a pathway to sustainability in a business. You're still trying to figure that out."

In early 2017, sales were down at both Gravity and ChargeItPro. The call center at ChargeItPro was having issues with long hold times and low service levels. As I'd feared, Phil's top-down management style had left his employees disempowered. Despite these challenges, I suspected the team had potential. They wanted to do the right things. They wanted to work hard, but no one had ever given them the opportunity. It was our responsibility to set them free and give them the autonomy to turn the company around.

I spoke with every ChargeItPro employee one-on-one. I found that many were just scraping by financially. Several were supporting families and were one unexpected expense away from losing their houses, their cars, and, as a result, their jobs. For them, the situation was dire.

In the face of conflicting opinions about how to proceed, I stalled. When I had raised salaries at Gravity, I was confident in the team's abilities. I knew they deserved to make more. I knew how hard they were working and how much they were sacrificing for our clients. I didn't even know if everyone on the ChargeItPro team was a good fit, long-term, for Gravity. I hadn't yet had the chance to determine if these new employees fit that same mold. What signal would I send if I gave someone a raise and then fired them the next day?

I kept hearing more stories from ChargeItPro employees. One man was supporting a wife and a child, teetering on the brink of financial implosion. Every pay period, he would stock up on food for his son. Once that food was purchased, he and his wife would buy their own food. If they ran out, they ate their son's leftovers until the next payday. Even the support team's supervisor was terrified of not being able to pay the mortgage on a modest home he had recently purchased. He was desperate, but he told me, "Don't raise our pay until you can afford it." It was powerful to hear him say something so selfless, but it was clear their minds weren't on work when they were so stressed in their personal lives. I knew we could do better.

I looked at what the company could afford. I knew ChargeItPro couldn't afford a $70,000 minimum wage right away. I thought $40,000 was a reasonable place to start for Idaho, and we just might be able to afford it. A $40,000 minimum-salary program would wipe out a significant amount of the current company profits. It would also make growth more expensive, since new hires would enter the company at this level. Our loan payments, which topped $200,000 every month, would also be difficult to afford. If we raised the minimum wage to $40,000, Gravity would need to subsidize the cost, an unsustainable situation that made me uncomfortable. With every passing pay period, I became more and more uneasy about the financial pain I was inflicting on the team at ChargeItPro. It was time to act.

I thought about all the arguments against raising salaries. They were all valid, but they also felt wrong. I couldn't put my finger on it, but I had the same feeling I had felt back in 2011 when deciding to implement our initial aggressive raise policy. Was raising salaries the rational thing to do? Was it in keeping with maximizing profits to ensure the company would continue to thrive? Definitely not in the short term, but I knew we would find a way to make it work. *I* would find a way to make it work.

In the summer of 2017, I informed my executive team that we would raise the minimum salary at ChargeItPro to $40,000, and we would work on a plan to get it to $70,000. Under this new policy, twenty people would receive raises of as much as 43 percent immediately. In September, I invited every member of the ChargeItPro team and their families to McCall, Idaho, for an off-site strategic-planning meeting. We spent time together, bonded over drinks, and met each other's kids, spouses, and parents. It was a magical weekend.

At the end of our time together, the entire group convened in a room at the Shore Lodge on Payette Lake. After a group discussion about the type of company we wanted to build, I took the floor. "When I look at all these kids and all these families, I don't see a single person who I would not want to be making enough to live—pay the bills, have a family, have all the basics in life covered," I said. "Our starting wage right now is right above the poverty line, and I haven't met anyone here who doesn't deserve more than that. I want everyone to work with your manager to put together a well-defined path to get to seventy thousand dollars, but I also can't live for one more day under our current system. So, starting today, we have a new floor of forty thousand dollars."

The room immediately erupted in applause. Marcus, on the tech support team, and Panida, on the accounting team, welled up. I wanted to enjoy the moment, but I knew there were people in the audience with conflicted emotions. I spoke louder over the applause and conversations taking place. "Now, if you're at forty-one thousand dollars, you probably feel completely shafted right now. So please come find me, and let's work on a plan to make it up to you. I know it's unfair, and I want to acknowledge that." Sarah, on the operations team, was fighting back tears. I asked her to speak. "It's life changing, it really is. It makes a huge difference. I'm a single mom with no other support besides my income right now. So times have been difficult, and again, it's life changing; it's a huge boost. Thank you." I felt the same joy I had felt announcing the original $70k policy at Gravity, but I also felt the pressure of additional weight on my shoulders.

Although the years immediately following the acquisition were challenging, they were also incredibly exciting. As with any merger, it can be difficult to integrate two teams, especially when those teams come from different backgrounds. Not only was the ChargeItPro management style far more traditional than Gravity's, but Boise is a comparatively more conservative place, socially and politically, than Seattle. To help with the transition, we appointed the head of our installation team, Jose, to act as a liaison between the two offices. He relocated to Boise and began talking to the team about their concerns, needs, and ideas. Our COO Tammi and I also made frequent trips to Boise, as did Rosita, who now headed our sales department. We felt it was important to promote unity while simultaneously encouraging diversity and believed our different opinions and perspectives would only make our culture stronger, even if it created tension at times.

The bigger challenge was making sure everyone performed at the same level. Phil had been notoriously reticent about addressing underperformers, a fact that not only cost the company money but reduced morale among team members who had to pick up the slack. Although we resisted the mass layoffs so typical of corporate acquisitions, our new pay policy forced us to hold people to a higher standard. While we had to ask a few people to leave, most of those who left ChargeItPro during this time did so voluntarily once they realized the new culture and way of approaching the business wasn't working for them.

Fortunately, most ChargeItPro employees welcomed the changes, especially our "be your own CEO" philosophy. Stifled for so long by Phil's old-school bureaucratic management style, they felt invigorated by their newfound autonomy. Not only did Gravity's flexible work arrangements allow them to do their work and live their lives in ways that were productive and satisfying for them, they seized opportunities to suggest ideas and make improvements. Several employees took on new and expanded roles and made changes that had an immediate positive impact on the company.

Meanwhile, Gravity has invested heavily in the ChargeItPro product and business model. As technology improves, more small businesses are looking for software that allows them to do more with less, whether it's accepting payments, keeping track of inventory, or securing customer information. By partnering with software companies who build these products and offering them seamless tools for their small-business customers to accept payments online and in-store, Gravity can offer our merchants an even better product. In the two years immediately following the acquisition, we looked at the ways our industry was changing and asked our team members—especially those in customer-facing sales and support roles—for feedback. We saw the potential in shifting our focus slightly and decided to invest heavily in improving our technology and partner relationships. We hired several talented developers and trained Gravity sales reps on the ChargeItPro product and partnership model. The hiring spree ate into profits, and the changes to our sales teams and selling process disrupted some procedures, but we believed this long-term investment strategy would pay off.

As we approached the second anniversary of the acquisition, we realized that, given the teamwork between Gravity and ChargeItPro, it made sense for us to fully merge into one company. Up until that point, ChargeItPro was structured as a subsidiary of Gravity, a separate legal and financial entity with its own branding and systems. Integrating the two companies would be complex and disruptive, but both teams expressed so much support for doing so that, in early 2019, we decided to make becoming one a priority.

We assembled a team of people from across the company to make a plan and oversee its execution. Tasks ranged from merging our payroll systems to creating unified branding to informing all ChargeItPro clients of the impending change. We'd also purchased a brand-new office space in downtown Boise and begun the process of renovating it inside and out. Several employees took on responsibility for overseeing the design and build-out with the goal of moving the ChargeItPro team in by the end of the year.

One of the biggest questions, of course, was whether to transition ChargeItPro employees to our $70k minimum wage. While only a few of them were earning the $40,000 minimum, most were earning less than $70,000. If we brought them into the fold and didn't pay them $70,000, we'd be reneging on our promise to pay all employees at least that much. However, ramping them up to $70,000 overnight would be a huge financial risk given our current expenses, not to mention the debt we'd acquired in purchasing the company. Plus, it could limit our ability to grow and invest in our technology, which would make us less competitive.

James, the head of Team Advocates (our human resources team), and Ian, our HR manager in Boise, reached out to me,

Tammi, and our head of finance, Edwin, to figure out a strategy. For several months, we considered moving away from the $70k minimum and toward a dynamic living-wage policy wherein we would pay a different minimum salary in different markets. Gravity employs people in roughly a dozen locations around the country, each of which has a vastly different cost of living. In addition to our main offices in Seattle and Boise, we have people in Hawaii, California, New York, Oregon, Oklahoma, Iowa, and Nebraska, among other areas, and we regularly hire remote employees in new locations. Since our goal with the $70k minimum was always to ensure our people made a living wage, we could calculate the living wage in each of these markets and set that as our minimum for those team members. Over time, we could adjust these numbers to account for changes in the cost of living, ensuring that no one was left behind. Plus, in a few of our markets, like California, Hawaii, and New York, $70,000 went much less far than it did in other places. Even in Seattle, it was hardly enough to achieve a middle-class lifestyle free from the burden of financial stress.

Ultimately, however, we decided to keep our current policy in place. There were several practical reasons for this. For one, setting one company-wide minimum would create less confusion. We wouldn't have to calculate salaries for different markets, nor would we have to adjust them regularly to keep up with rising costs. And even though the initial $70k story was four years old, people still knew us as the company with a $70k minimum wage. How would we explain to new applicants that was no longer the case? Plus, by definition, a living wage is different not only for different markets but for different people. Would we pay a single person with no dependents the same as the only working adult in a family of four? Would we increase someone's pay when they had children or got a divorce? Would we reduce someone's salary if they moved from Seattle to Boise?

But the real reason we decided to double down on $70k was that we knew it was worth it. Even though that salary would go farther in Boise than in Seattle, the ChargeItPro team had consistently proven they could punch above their weight and add the same amount of value as anyone at Gravity. Having a high minimum salary is an extension of our "be your own CEO" culture. By giving each and every team member the autonomy and trust to make important decisions on behalf of the company, we endow them with a great responsibility—responsibility that in other companies might be reserved for people with specific titles or roles. For the past two-plus years, our Boise team members had proven themselves not only willing but eager to be their own CEOs. They deserved a salary that reflected their contributions.

In September 2019, I announced the new policy at the opening of our new Boise office. We'd been working to open this office for the better part of a year and were marking the occasion with a formal opening ceremony and celebration. This new building symbolized our commitment to the area and our people there. Announcing the wage at the same time as we welcomed our Boise team to their new home felt like the perfect way to mark the occasion of our two companies finally becoming one.

As we had done in Seattle, we would roll out the new wage over the course of a few years. Effective immediately, anyone earning less than $50,000 a year would be bumped up to that level; employees earning between $50,000 and $70,000 would receive a small raise decided by their manager. Starting January 1, 2021, the minimum would increase by $5,000 each year until hitting $70,000 in 2024.

On the morning of Monday, September 23, 2019, our Boise team members, along with a few people from the Seattle office, assembled in the parking lot of the new building. It was a clear, gorgeous early-fall day, and there was a hum of excitement in the air as everyone anxiously awaited the opportunity to settle into their new workspaces. My ninety-three-year-old grandmother was there, and I'd spent the previous night at my parents' house a few minutes away. Being in Idaho again felt simultaneously like a homecoming and a new beginning. I as a person and Gravity as a company had grown and changed vastly over the past fifteen years. And yet, we'd never lost sight of our roots.

After a few minutes of mingling, longtime ChargeItPro sales rep Dan O'Bannon stood in front of the crowd and said a few words about how he believed the coming together of our two companies would make us all stronger and more resilient in the future. Then he welcomed me to the mic. I exchanged places with Dan and began to speak about how far we had come as a company and how excited I was to see what we would accomplish in the future. I spoke about how Gravity and ChargeItPro were both founded on a similar set of principles and had dedicated themselves to helping independent business owners succeed. I spoke about coming together as one, and how that unity had helped us provide even better service to our customers. And, finally, I spoke about how we needed to support our employees so we could continue to thrive.

"What I want to build, all together, is a support system for these independent businesses, where we really believe in them, work for them, sacrifice for them and also for each other," I said. "There's been a pretty big debate back and forth about pay equality and pay equity and living wage and all those sorts of things in the company over the past several weeks, and how are we going to think about Idaho and the legacy of Gravity and the living wage of Gravity and everything. And I'm here to announce to you today that we're going to be putting a scaled policy into place and between now and 2024, we're going to be implementing a seventy-thousand-dollar minimum wage for everybody at Gravity, everybody coming from ChargeItPro here as well."

Unlike four years prior, when our Seattle team had initially reacted to this news with stunned silence, the crowd in Boise immediately erupted into applause and cheers. Several people hugged and high-fived me, and a few began sharing their stories.

One of our tech support analysts, Nick Varner, gave an interview to the local NBC affiliate KTVB, whom we'd invited to attend the event. "I just got custody of my boys, got them out of a bad situation," he said. "It's a game-changer." Nick had joined the company earlier that year, and hearing his story reminded me, yet again, how big of a difference even a few thousand dollars can make to someone's quality of life.

But the story was far from over. The next morning, the office opening and wage announcement had made the front page of the *Idaho Statesman*, complete with a photo of the whole team standing in front of the new building. Much as the original announcement had four-and-a-half years prior, the news took off. Within a few days, the story appeared in online outlets all over the world, including CNN, ABC News, Today.com, and the *Daily Mail*. Fox Business invited me to debate our wage policy on air—twice—mostly using our example to defend private-sector solutions to income inequality in America. We started trending on Reddit, and emails once again started flooding every inbox we had. They came from job seekers, business owners, reporters, and regular people wanting to wish us well.

While it was exciting to see the story resonate and get some attention for our Boise team, I also couldn't help feeling a little saddened by how many people found it noteworthy. When we first announced the $70k wage in 2015, I'd hoped to serve as an example to others that you could run a sustainable business while still paying people well. I'd hoped other businesses would follow suit, or perhaps come up with a different policy that could have an even bigger impact. While some did, the big picture has gone from bad to worse. Three days after the Boise story hit, the US Census Bureau released new data showing that

American income inequality was the highest it had been in five decades.[6] If we keep on this trajectory, we will soon live in a world where a handful of people control most of the world's wealth—a scenario in which the rest of us will essentially be dependent on the wealthy, who can use their money to buy influence and consolidate power. Despite our success as a company, the relative lack of social and economic progress has made me wonder what must happen to effect change on a systemic scale. I don't know the answer right now. All I know is that I'm not finished trying to figure it out.

6. Taylor Telford, "Income Inequality in America Is the Highest It's Been Since Census Bureau Started Tracking It, Data Shows," *Washington Post*, September 26, 2019, https://www.washingtonpost.com/business/2019/09/26/income-inequality-america-highest-its-been-since-census-started-tracking-it-data-show/.

Epilogue

IN MARCH 2019, a few weeks shy of the fourth anniversary of our $70k decision, Nicholas Kristof, one of the most respected columnists at the *New York Times*, reached out to me via Twitter to ask if he could profile Gravity. Although no one at Gravity had ever spoken to Nick directly, he remembered our story and had heard from various sources that our living-wage policy had been successful. He asked if he could come to Seattle to find out for himself.

When he arrived at our office a few days later, he met with me, Tammi, and several people from the team whose lives had been directly affected by the policy. Each of us shared our stories and impressions about how the policy had affected the company. We also provided statistics about how our business has fared since the policy went into effect. Processing volume—a key metric used in the payments industry to measure growth—had increased by more than 160 percent, and our client base had grown by more than 75 percent. Our headcount had increased by roughly 70 percent—from 120 to 200 employees—while our employee turnover had dropped from an annual average of 40 to 60 percent to 15 to 30 percent. Although we'll never know what these numbers would have looked like if we had continued to pay market-rate wages, we can say for certain that paying a living wage has not crippled our business as some early observers predicted.

Nick was particularly interested in the human impact of our decision. After all, my key reason for raising wages had been to improve employee well-being and reduce the stress of having to worry about money. Had I succeeded?

Based on the data we gathered in 2016 (which I shared in chapter 14), we knew the policy had had an immediate positive impact, but a lot had changed since then. Many people had joined the company in that time, and many of our more experienced employees had taken pay cuts to join us because, like Tammi, they saw opportunity in working for a smaller company that aligned with their values and where they could take on more responsibility. How had those new employees fared?

To find out, we looked at personnel records and sent a survey to everyone to gather new data. The results confirmed what we already knew anecdotally. More than 10 percent of our team members said they had purchased their first home since the policy went into effect. This is an impressive feat considering that Seattle has one of the most expensive housing markets in the country and the cost of living in many of our markets— including Boise, one of the country's fastest-growing cities—

continues to rise. Individual 401(k) contributions had more than doubled, and more than 70 percent of employees with debt reported being able to pay a portion of it down. More than a third of those with debt had been able to pay it down by 50 percent or more.

I'm happy to report that our baby boom has continued in earnest. We now average roughly eight new births per year, and thanks to our open-paid-time-off policy, which went into effect in 2014, Gravity parents have more time available to spend with their ever-expanding families.

Many respondents reported other improvements such as taking nicer or more frequent vacations, eating more healthfully, moving closer to work and/or to a nicer neighborhood, getting married, going back to school, joining a gym, or spending more time and money on their favorite hobbies. These responses indicate that our employees now have the freedom to make choices that are right for them without having to sacrifice other aspects of their lives. Parents don't have to choose between paying for childcare or leaving the workforce to stay at home with their kids. They don't have to give up memory-making family vacations in order to move to a better school district. They don't have to forgo their own hobbies in order to enroll their kids in music or sports lessons. They don't have to put off saving for retirement in order to save for their kids' educations. Younger workers don't have to live in an unsafe neighborhood or shoddy apartment in order to pay off their student loans. They don't have to skip doctor appointments because they need to pay for car repairs. They don't have to work a second full-time job at McDonald's, as Rosita once did, in order to afford to live.

The numbers speak for themselves, but what struck me the most about the survey responses were the direct testimonials from individuals about how the policy had impacted their lives.

"When the living wage went into effect, I personally owned a foam mattress, a desk, and a dog that had to live with my ex-girlfriend until I could afford living in a place that would allow me to have a dog," wrote one employee. "Two months later, we moved, and I got my dog back. [I] turned the foam mattress into a dog bed and got a real mattress. . . . The living wage increased my quality of life dramatically."

"From a high level," wrote another, "my comp at Gravity has allowed me to make decisions for the right reasons (values) as opposed to being limited by what I can afford."

"There is a certain level of stress that comes with not making a living wage," said another. "The idea that a flat tire could mean you can't afford rent or will be eating ramen or other low cost/ low nutrition food [is stressful]. Without that stress I feel like I am reclaiming my life. I am able to take care of myself and my health. I wake up each day happier and am making plans to purchase my first home."

Even people whose salaries did not increase spoke about how working at Gravity had had a positive impact on their lives:

"The [living] wage didn't greatly affect me in particular. I moved from a high-paying position to this one. But I can see the difference in the dedication the employees have [here] vs [at] my old company. The employees here tend to go above and beyond, and I do think that has something to do with the wage. They feel like they are getting paid a fair wage so they should do the job to the best ability that they can."

"I make less here than I used to, but am accepted, which is hard to put a price tag on."

"While I wasn't directly impacted by the living wage policy, I really enjoy and appreciate the caliber of people I get to work with each day. I'm happy knowing that they are being taken care of financially and that they have fewer financial distractions to deal with."

I don't pretend that our policy has eradicated all the stress that comes with living in America today. We still live in a society where one medical emergency can wipe out someone's life savings and oppressive student-loan payments can deplete even a relatively large paycheck each month. I also know that the cost of living in America is rising so quickly that $70,000 is no longer enough to achieve a comfortable middle-class lifestyle for many people. I know that we as a society and Gravity as a company still have a long way to go to right the wrongs of modern capitalism, but the fact that one decision has been able to have such a huge positive impact on so many people gives me hope that things can change.

The final *Times* column was extremely positive. "Gravity shows that at least for some companies in some industries, it is possible to thrive while treating even the lowest-level workers with dignity," Nick wrote. "And that's not the death of capitalism but perhaps part of its rebirth." Having weathered my share of negative press, I felt gratified by having a respected journalist give an honest account of our story. We, as a company, had decided not to focus on PR for the past few years because we knew the best way to prove our critics wrong was to ignore them, put our heads down, and do the job we're in business to do. Our customers don't care how many magazines write about us or what Fox News or the *New York Times* says about my management decisions. What has helped our business thrive since we enacted our living-wage policy is the same thing that helped us thrive before: providing incredible customer service to our merchants.

Still, I understand why outsiders are curious about how we've been doing. I can share revenue and attrition statistics until I'm blue in the face, but people will always wonder whether it's just PR spin. To have an unbiased third party deem us successful doesn't change who we are, but it does signal something positive to those who would doubt us.

At the same time, this sort of attention makes me wonder about the traditional definition of corporate success. Yes, a business has to make money in order to stay in business, but so many people measure a company's success solely by how much money it makes or how high its stock price is that day. By this standard, many people would have labeled us unsuccessful if our $70k policy had caused us to make less money, even if it improved our employees' lives.

I take issue with this definition. Profit cannot and should not be the only measure of a company's success. This line of thinking has led to some of the most intractable crises facing our society today, from man-made climate change to unprecedented income inequality. We have allowed business leaders to abdicate all responsibility except for satisfying shareholders, to the point that anyone who seeks to do things differently is accused of being antibusiness, un-American, and a threat to our way of life.

One need not look far for an example. In late 2018, Amazon caused an uproar when it announced it would open two new headquarters in Arlington, Virginia, and Long Island City, New York. For over a year, Amazon had pitted dozens of municipalities against one another as they vied for the fifty thousand new jobs the company promised it would bring to whatever location it selected. When Amazon announced it would split the majority of those jobs between a DC suburb and a rapidly gentrifying neighborhood in Queens, they were met with mixed reactions.

While some Virginians and New Yorkers were excited by the prospect of so many new jobs coming to their area, others were dismayed by how one of the world's most valuable companies had negotiated billions of dollars in tax incentives without involving residents and certain local elected officials in the decision-making process. A few months later, after some Queens politicians voiced opposition to the deal and demanded more accountability from Amazon, Amazon abruptly backed out. "The commitment to build a new headquarters requires positive, collaborative relationships with state and local elected officials who will be supportive over the long-term," the company announced in a public statement. The fact that Amazon chose to renege on the deal without meeting with opponents or negotiating openly and in good faith is telling. It suggests that, in the minds of its executives, Amazon's right to do business where and how it pleases is more important than the concerns of millions of residents and taxpayers whose lives will be directly affected by the company's presence in their backyard. It's perhaps even more telling that New York governor Andrew Cuomo, who said he was blindsided by Amazon's decision to back out of the state, immediately tried to convince them to change their minds.

Another illustrative example of this entitlement can be seen in the testimony J. P. Morgan Chase CEO Jamie Dimon gave to the House Committee on Financial Services in April 2019. Representative Katie Porter of California told Dimon about a Chase employee in Irvine, California, who earns $2,425 a month. A single mother, this employee ends each month with a $567 deficit after paying for basic expenses like rent, childcare, utilities, groceries, and gas. "My question for you, Mr. Dimon," Congresswoman Porter asked, "is how should she manage this budget shortfall while she's working full-time at your bank?"

Dimon, who earned $31 million in compensation in 2018, answered, "I don't know. I'd have to think about that."

"Would you recommend that she take out a J. P. Morgan Chase credit card and run a deficit?" Porter asked.

"I don't know. I'd have to think about it."

"Would you recommend that she overdraft at your bank and be charged overdraft fees?"

"I don't know. I'd have to think about it."

We have become so used to the idea that the richest executives earn more money than they can spend while the poorest among us cannot afford to feed and clothe their children that even though Dimon's response is appalling, it is not surprising. Even advocates of higher pay would have been shocked if Dimon had said Chase should pay its employees a living wage, instead of equivocating and refusing to answer the question. We've become so accustomed to executives justifying low salaries in the name of staying competitive and generating shareholder value that we forget that American capitalism used to be very different.

Until the 1970s, when Milton Friedman declared that a business's main purpose is to provide returns to shareholders, and the 1980s, when Ronald Reagan popularized the notion of trickle-down economics, the most successful American corporations considered it their responsibility to take care of their employees, customers, and communities while trying to remain innovative and profitable. The brand of capitalism that made the United States the wealthiest country in the world and helped create a vibrant middle class bears little resemblance to the capitalism at work in America today.

Gerard Swope, the president of General Electric from 1922 to 1940, summed up this idea during a cross-country tour shortly after he took the reins of the company. "There are three factors in our economic system today that must be taken into consideration in our work: the shareholders, the employees, the community," Swope told GE's foremen. Pointing to the financial health of the company, Swope declared that he wasn't worried about the commitment to shareholders but added, "My greatest concern is in the other two phases of our responsibility, that towards the employee and to the community at large. As to the employees, I infer every man here realizes that he is dealing with men and not with material or machinery. In our human relations between employees and employers there must be justice and sympathy. We spend so much of our time, so much of our life, in industry that we can get a very much greater satisfaction out of life if we have the conditions which surround our work pleasant and congenial."[22]

Swope was not alone in his thinking. In his excellent book *The End of Loyalty* (from which the above anecdote is taken), management expert Rick Wartzman discusses how for the first half of the twentieth century, the heads of four of America's largest, most innovative, and most powerful companies—

---

7. Rick Wartzman, *The End of Loyalty: The Rise and Fall of Good Jobs in America* (New York: PublicAffairs, 2017), 30.

GE, General Motors, Kodak, and Coca-Cola—took care of employees. They provided comfortable salaries and generous pensions while negotiating in good faith with unions to protect the rights and safety of all workers.

Compare that to the leadership style of Jack Welch, who took over as GE's chairman and CEO in 1981. Welch became notorious after instituting his so-called "rank and yank" policy, under which he fired the lowest-performing 10 percent of GE workers every year. It's hard to imagine Gerard Swope adopting such a policy, but because of the business environment of the 1980s—characterized by increasing globalization, rapidly changing technology, and an overwhelming pressure to protect and expand market share—Welch was hailed as a hero and an innovator who helped transform GE into a twenty-first-century success.

Plenty has been written about why and how this evolution—or devolution—took place. If you're interested in a more in-depth account, I highly recommend *The End of Loyalty*, as well as the work of Robert Reich[7] and Steven Pearlstein, both of whom trace the history of capitalism in America in a much more thorough and erudite way than I ever could. I mention the trend here only to remind people that our attitudes about business have evolved and can continue to evolve if we want them to. The only thing we need is the will to change.

And that change starts with you and me. I used to believe that a business's sole purpose was to help customers. It was only after I started my own business and realized how many other people were affected by my decisions that I came to understand the full extent of my responsibility. I used to think that as long as we were making money, we were successful. But when I learned that the people who were helping us make that money were struggling, I knew I had to expand my definition of success. If Gravity went out of business tomorrow, I know that a lot of people would say we had failed. By the traditional definition, they might be right. But when I read the testimonials from the employees whose lives improved by working here, or the business owners who started paying their employees more after hearing our example, or the leaders who chose to follow their values instead of focusing solely on making money, I know our success can't be measured in dollars alone. And I know that every sacrifice I as a CEO and we as a company have made has been worth it.

Acknowledgments

I would like to thank the following individuals for supporting this book in its earliest days:

Adam Mutschler

Alexander Pusch

Andrea Rodriguez

Angela Montgomery

Anisha Chhetri

Betta Beasley

Blas Pegenaute

Bobbie Austin

Bobby Powers

Bojan Dimitrijevic

Brian Urban

Cameron Mitchell

Christina Stone

Christine Sigglin

Colin Dow

Daniel Reed

Dennis Aranda

Diana Kviatkovskaja

Douglas Browne

Dustin Wilmoth

Ed & Karyn Pallay

Elizabeth Ringwald

Gerald Carter

Grace Moon

Gregg Gies

Gwendolyn Monangai

Jalila Al-Khalil

James Wickey

Jean Ali Muhlbauer

Jin Yoo

Jon Andrew

Josh Arnold

Julia Lucero

Justin Fogle

Katie DiJulio

Kris M. Clark

Leah Calo

Leigh Nolan

Lindsay O'Shea

Maksim Mikossyanchik

Mandy McGill

Mario Crea

Marva Whitaker

Maureen Rodriguez

Mike Ebbers

Nick Santora

Oksana Lukash

Pamala Warren

Panu Luukka

Patrick Gleeson

Patrick Kennedy

Paul Hamaishi

Richard Clarke

Richard Geoffroy

Sherry Nelson

Stanislav Feoktistov

Ted Biele

Thomas Kempf

Tola Kong

Vihan Khanna

William Perlman

Yves Cavarec

Appendix 1

How to Pay a Living Wage

WHEN I SHARE OUR living-wage story, people typically respond with some version of the same question: "How can I do something similar at my organization?"

Sometimes they ask because they are eager to create change and are looking for suggestions about how to implement or improve their compensation policies. They are committed to paying their people more but aren't sure how to do so in a way that won't destroy their business, create tension among their team, or anger shareholders.

Other times when people ask this question, it's meant to be rhetorical and is usually followed by some sort of excuse: "How can I do something similar at my organization when . . . I'm beholden to investors? . . . it would cut into profits that could be put back into our company? . . . our margins are too thin? . . . higher wages could decrease productivity?" and so on.

These questions don't surprise me. The people who ask

them have been taught—as I was in my early days of being an entrepreneur—that a business exists solely to make money and that anyone who believes differently is stupid and/or naïve.

I also know that, for skeptics, it's not enough for me to tell the story of how Gravity has thrived because of our living-wage policy. "Your business is different from mine," they protest. "Just because you made it work doesn't mean anyone can."

That may or may not be true, but, ultimately, these are just excuses. The real reason people resist paying a living wage is because they're afraid. They might be afraid for different reasons—some are afraid of going against the grain, some are afraid of giving up their profits, some are afraid of going out of business—but they're all afraid. I know this fear all too well, but I also know that nothing of consequence was ever accomplished without someone taking a risk. Fear is not an excuse for accepting the status quo when the status quo actively harms so many people.

The truth is not only *can* businesses succeed by paying people more, they *must* do whatever they can to offer a living wage to their employees. If they don't, the ultrawealthy will come to control our society even more than they already do. Businesses that don't already dominate their markets will be pushed out of them, and the customers they depend on will no longer be able to afford their services. Paying a living wage is not something you should wait to do until it's convenient or safe. You should start doing whatever you can today.

Of course, every business is different. Many companies

could afford to pay a $70,000 minimum wage if they chose to, but that will not be possible, or even desirable, for everyone. What is right for you depends on the needs of your company and its employees, and how you choose to implement it should ultimately be up to you. To provide some guidance and hopefully inspire you to get started, this appendix will help you figure out how to pay your people more. Whether you're the CEO of a Fortune 500 company, a small business owner operating on razor-thin margins, or an employee who wants to start earning enough to live a decent, less-stressful life, there are things you can start doing today to help get you to your goals, even if you have to start small.

What Is a Living Wage?

Before you implement a new wage policy, you need to figure out what a living wage is for your area. I chose $70,000 as our living wage because it was right for our company and our people at the time. But living wages are different for different people and depend on factors like location, age, family size, and living expenses.

To determine what a living wage is for your area, a good place to start is the MIT Living Wage Calculator, which can be accessed online at livingwage.mit.edu. This calculator allows you to look up what an individual needs to earn per hour (based on a forty-hour work week) in order to cover the basic expenses like housing, food, health care, transportation, and childcare. It also breaks down wages for different household sizes in order to account for variance in living expenses. For example, the living wage for an unmarried person with no dependents is less than that of a single parent of two kids living in the same area.

The calculator, however, does not factor in things like entertainment or vacations, which help us live joyful, interesting lives, or savings, which allows us to alleviate the stress that comes from an unexpected expense or planning for the future. For this reason, I would expand the definition of a living wage to include enough income for regular travel, hobbies, nights out, and occasional other diversions. These items are not "necessities" per se, but they are essential for promoting well-being and giving people a chance to recharge from the daily demands of work, commuting, childcare, paying bills, and getting food on the table.

A true living wage should also allow people to save at least 10 percent of their gross income for emergency expenses and retirement and another 10 percent to donate a portion of their income to causes or organizations that are important to them. Taken together, these expenditures help strengthen relationships and alleviate stress, which improves health and therefore makes people better able to participate in their communities.

Taking all of this into account, you should add about 20 to 30 percent to the figures provided by the MIT calculator when determining a living wage for your area. Remember that this is a starting point and that different people will have different needs. If you are serious about paying a living wage at your organization, it's worth talking to as many people who will be affected as possible to figure out what would work best.

Once you have a sense of the wage you want to work toward, you need to determine the best way to make that wage possible. In the sections that follow, I'll provide guidelines for figuring this out on your own, but ultimately the path you choose is up to you. Even if you're not in a position to do something drastic, you can still have an impact. The important thing is that you're willing to take a risk to accomplish the change you seek. When you demonstrate sacrifice, people will know you're serious and will be more willing to follow your lead.

What Can Employees Do?

We tend to assume employees have relatively little power over wages, since they depend on their employers to set their salaries. But individually and together, employees can have tremendous influence over how wages are determined at their organizations. Traditionally, the most effective way employees have been able to control how much they earn was through unions, and the decline of unions over the second half of the twentieth century has been correlated with the rise of income inequality in America.[8] Unfortunately, our recent love affair

---

8. Economic Policy Institute, https://www.epi.org/news/union-member-ship-declines-inequality-rises/, accessed December 4, 2019

with deregulation brought with it a slew of anti-union laws that limit collective bargaining in many areas, making it more difficult for workers, particularly blue-collar workers, to demand higher wages. But even within this new reality, there are things you can do to promote a living wage for yourself and your coworkers.

The easiest place to start is with your own salary. If you are not already earning a living wage, make doing so a priority. We've grown accustomed to the idea that certain professions should not pay as much as others or that employers should only be responsible for paying people whatever the market says they're worth, even if that number is well below what it takes to live. We've also come to believe that certain people can earn less because they work in fields that reward them in other ways—think of the starving artist who has sacrificed material comforts in order to pursue his creative passions, or the nonprofit worker who accepts a lifetime of relatively low pay for the chance to do what she considers meaningful work.

Whether you earn less than a living wage because you've chosen to or not, you need to recognize the trade-offs you're making when you can't afford the basics. Maybe you're content living in a shabby apartment, driving a beat-up car, or eating in every night, but if you can't afford to stay in that apartment when the landlord jacks up the rent or to pay for a new transmission when your old one finally dies, you are sacrificing your mental and physical health and well-being by having to worry about money. Wanting to earn a living wage does not make you materialistic or greedy. It simply makes you a human being with the same basic needs as every other human being.

Calculate Your Needs

The first step toward earning a living wage is to figure out what a living wage is for someone in your situation. You can use the MIT calculator to help you figure this out based on your location and general expenses, but it would be more accurate to calculate the number for yourself. There are many great personal-finance books and budgeting tools that can help you do this. Essentially, you just need to figure out how much you spend each year on things like rent/mortgage, bills, childcare, loan payments, food, transportation, prescriptions/doctor visits, insurance, and anything else you can't cut from your budget without negative consequences. If expenses fluctuate from month to month—for instance, you probably don't spend the same amount on clothing every month—add up how much you spend each year and divide that number by twelve to get a monthly average. Add up the monthly averages for each category and multiply that number by twelve to arrive at your annual expenses. You should also factor in how much you pay in taxes. If you're not sure how much you pay, you can estimate based on last year's tax return, the figure provided in the MIT calculator, or the rates listed on the IRS website as well as those of your state and local treasury offices.

This will give you the gross annual income you need to earn

based on the traditional definition of a living wage. Now you want to factor in things like savings and extras you need so that you're not living a bare-bones existence. What hobbies bring you joy? How often do you need to take a vacation and travel to recharge? What are your favorite social activities that keep you connected to your friends and communities? How much would these activities add to your annual cost of living? Add this number to your previous total and divide this new number by 0.9. This will show you how much you need to earn in order to be able to save 10 percent of your income for the future or emergencies.

I'd also encourage you to think long-term and figure out what you'd need to earn in the future in order to build the life you want. Do you want to have kids? Get married? Move to a better neighborhood or home? Help support your aging parents? Do you want to switch careers, and will that require you to get a degree or move to a different city? How much will your income need to grow in five, ten, or twenty years in order to meet these goals? Even if you don't know exactly how much all of this will cost or you're still figuring out your plans for the future, knowing how much you might need will allow you to set income goals that you can work toward over time.

Make a Plan

If you're already earning a living wage, congratulations. If not, make a plan to get there as quickly as possible. The first step is the most obvious and, for many, the most intimidating: talk to your boss. Many people delay having these conversations until they have some leverage, like another job offer or a favorable performance review. But one of the ways to educate people about the need for a living wage is to have frank, honest conversations about money. Studies show that three out of five people do not negotiate their salaries when accepting a new job offer, and the rate is even lower for women.[9] By some measures, this failure to negotiate leads the average employee to earn a current annual base salary of $7,500 less than they could.[10] Luckily, thanks to the rise of websites like Glassdoor and PayScale, there are plenty of resources available to help you determine the salary range for your industry or position.

Tell your boss you want to have a meeting to discuss your compensation goals and role within the company. Make sure to give yourself enough time to have the conversation—an hour should be ideal to start—and give your boss enough time to prepare. Try to pick a time when your boss is usually relaxed—for example, a Friday morning instead of a Monday morning, or soon after she's completed a major meeting or trip and has some downtime in her schedule.

---

9. Glassdoor, "3 in 5 Employees Did Not Negotiate Salary," May 2, 2016, https://www.glassdoor.com/blog/3-5-u-s-employees-negotiate-salary/.

10. Emily Moore, "Should You Always Negotiate Your Salary?" Glassdoor, September 21, 2018, https://www.glassdoor.com/blog/should-you-always-negotiate-your-salary/.

There are tons of resources on how to negotiate effectively. Ultimately, though, good negotiation comes down to remembering Stephen Covey's fourth habit: "Think win-win." While I hope we will soon live in a world where managers want to pay their employees a living wage because it is the right thing to do, you can always marshal data about the tangible benefits of a living wage if you're met with resistance. At Gravity, we often reference the work of Daniel Pink, whose book *Drive* discusses what really motivates people to work hard. Pink's research shows that, while money rarely motivates people to work harder, *not* having enough money is inherently demotivating because it turns people's focus away from the task at hand. You could also point to research that shows how people who earn a living wage are less stressed, sleep better, and are generally healthier than those who don't.[11] Given how much stress, sleep, and health are correlated with productivity, cognitive ability, and energy levels, your boss should understand the benefit of removing money as a stressor in your life. Don't be afraid to be honest with your boss about your financial situation. Many people feel uncomfortable showing this type of vulnerability in a negotiation, as they think it indicates weakness. But being honest with your boss helps establish trust and demonstrates that you want them to be part of the solution.

---

11. Matthew Desmond, "Dollars on the Margins," *New York Times Magazine,* February 26, 2019, https://www.nytimes.com/interactive/2019/02/21/magazine/minimum-wage-saving-lives.html.

If you're earning close to a living wage already and your performance has been good, you may be able to negotiate a raise effective immediately. If the difference is more than a few thousand dollars per year, you work for a smaller company with tighter margins, or the company is experiencing financial difficulty, you may have to work with your boss to figure out a longer-term plan for getting your salary where it needs to be. What positions in your organization pay at the level you're trying to reach? Are any of them aligned with your skills and career objectives? If so, what would it take for you to move into one of those roles? Is there an unmet need in the company or your department that you could fulfill? Are there any cost-cutting or revenue-generating projects you could tackle? Is there a skill you have or are looking to develop that the team could use? Maybe the marketing team is short-staffed and you could use your social-media skills to boost visibility. Or maybe you could put your bartending knowledge to work at the company holiday party, saving money on outside help. The possibilities are limited only by your imagination, and if you can demonstrate the value to your boss, it's highly likely he or she will be on board.

Ultimately, the best strategy is to be honest about your needs and goals while demonstrating your willingness to return the value of your salary to the company. Take it from a CEO who has had countless compensation conversations: if you can demonstrate that your desire for a higher salary comes from a legitimate desire to improve your life and you are open to working with your boss to figure out a path to get there, you will be poised to succeed.

What If Your Boss Says No?

There is always a chance that your boss will refuse to give you a raise. Whether this is for valid reasons (such as that the company can't afford it) or invalid ones (such as your boss justifying a low salary by citing market rates), you need to consider switching jobs if you don't see a path to earning a living wage at your current one. Luckily, thanks to increased awareness about income inequality and a low unemployment rate (at least at the time of this writing), many companies are realizing the value of paying more to attract talent. If you enjoy your job, it's likely you'll be able to find a better-paying one—or at least one with more growth opportunities—in your field.

Unfortunately, there are certain fields that simply don't pay a lot of money, especially for people who are early in their careers. This includes many jobs that provide incredibly valuable services to society, even though that value is not recognized through their pay. If you work in one of these professions, consider transitioning to a more lucrative field, even if it's just temporarily, in order to acquire skills that will make you successful in your dream career. For example, if you want to work in marketing for a nonprofit, you could work your way up through another organization—say, a marketing agency that works with nonprofits—and then transition to your dream job once you reach a level that commands a higher salary. Once there, you can become an advocate for higher pay for those at lower salary levels and use your influence and expertise to help drive change at the organization.

Bottom line: you shouldn't have to sacrifice your basic welfare in order to make a difference or do meaningful work. Although you might not currently be in a position to set your own or others' salaries, you can drive the conversation forward by setting an example and advocating for yourself. In the process, you'll also develop skills like negotiation and communication that will make you a more effective leader, no matter what line of work you're in.

Owners and Executives

If you're a business owner or executive, you are in the best position to implement immediate and meaningful change because you can do so relatively quickly. How you do this will depend on your leadership style, what industry you're in, how your company is structured, and how large it is. You should only make decisions you believe are right for your organization, but to help you get started, here is a basic framework.

What Do You Need to Pay?
Calculate a living wage for your employees using the tools described earlier in this chapter. To estimate their living

expenses, survey your workforce and/or work with your HR team to determine household size for those on the lower end of the pay scale. If there is no typical household size among your workforce, estimate your living wage based on a larger household size to ensure you're meeting most people's needs. Remember to add 20 to 30 percent for extras and savings. Be sure to calculate a living wage for each location where you have employees, since the cost of living can vary widely from city to city and state to state.

Once you have a working number for each area, figure out how many of your employees are earning less than that in their respective locations. How wide is the gap? How much would it cost to raise everyone's salaries to a living wage today? Are the gaps larger in certain regions or areas of the company? What about between demographics—are women or people of color earning less than their colleagues? What other trends do you see? Breaking down this data will allow you to identify areas that require the most immediate attention, which could be useful if you later determine you are not able to immediately institute a living wage across the board.

Close the Gap

The most straightforward way to bring everyone's salaries up is to draw on your company's profits to pay for the increase. Could you afford to raise everyone's salaries by accepting a lower annual profit margin? How much could you afford to pay employees and remain in the black? Work with your finance team to pencil out different scenarios and select the one with the biggest potential upside for employee wages, even if it comes at the expense of profits, shareholder dividends, or bonuses.

If you can't afford to bring everyone up to a living wage right now, consider what improvements you could make in the short term that would have the most impact on the most people. At Gravity, we rolled out the $70k policy over the course of three years. In 2015, when I made the announcement, we brought everyone up to at least $50,000. In 2016, the minimum went to $60,000, and in 2017, we finally reached $70,000. This way the increase had an immediate positive impact on over half of our employees without putting the company in a precarious position. Many companies have done something similar. For example, in April 2019, Target announced a $13-per-hour minimum wage, with the plan to increase that to $15 an hour by the end of 2020. That same month, Bank of America announced a similar move, raising its minimum wage to $17 an hour starting May 1, with the goal of getting to $20 an hour by 2021.

Another option is to look at groups within your company to see who stands to benefit the most from an increase and offer the largest and/or most immediate increases to them to start. What would it cost to close the minority or gender wage gap at your organization, assuming there is one? What would it cost to make pay more equitable between departments or increase wages for low-paid workers in areas with higher costs of living? Not only would fixing this disparity help the individuals at your company, it would also help them command higher salaries in future positions and potentially help drive wages up in your region or industry.

Reduce Inequality

Another way to afford a living wage is to reduce inequality between the highest and lowest earners. Even if you can afford to reduce your profit margin in order to pay people more, it's worth considering this strategy so you can put your profits to work in other ways.

Earlier in this book, I pointed out that the average CEO now earns 271 times more than their typical worker. In 1965, when America's gross domestic product (GDP) grew at a rate of 6.4 percent, compared to 2017's 2.3 percent, CEOs earned only 20 times more. What is the ratio of executive versus typical or average employee pay at your company? What would it look like to reduce—or at least freeze—executive compensation until everyone else earned a living wage?

What about Investors?

In the past fifty years or so, companies have become myopically focused on pleasing investors and shareholders. There are many reasons for this, most notably the relatively recent trend of paying a large percentage of executive salaries in the form of stocks and bonuses, both of which rise and fall based on short-term business performance. The result is that executives have been rewarded for delivering short-term gains even if they come at the expense of employees, the environment, public health, or the long-term sustainability of the company.

This focus on short-term profits has contributed to some of the worst crises in recent American history: the 2008 credit crisis and recession, the opioid epidemic that has claimed hundreds of thousands of American lives, Russian interference in our election through social media, the rise of unhealthful and potentially dangerous ingredients in our food and household products, climate change, and, of course, the rising inequality we've spent the better part of this book discussing.

Our economy has become so volatile that some of the most famous and successful investors are now urging the companies in which they invest to change course. In his 2019 letter to CEOs, BlackRock chairman and CEO Larry Fink stated point-blank that executives should stop making profit the sole purpose of business. "Purpose is not the sole pursuit of profits but the animating force for achieving them," he wrote. "Purpose unifies management, employees, and communities. It drives ethical behavior and creates an essential check on actions that go against the best interests of stakeholders. Purpose guides culture, provides a framework for consistent decision-making, and, ultimately, helps sustain long-term financial returns for the shareholders of your company."[12] Fink has become enormously wealthy by investing in profitable companies and is one of the most respected names in finance. If you're going to pay attention

---

12. Larry Fink, "Purpose and Profit," BlackRock, 2019, https://www.black-rock.com/corporate/investor-relations/larry-fink-ceo-letter.

to what investors think, he's a good investor to pay attention to.

Ignoring the short-term interests of investors does not mean you should ignore investors outright. Good leaders will communicate their vision, goals, and reasoning in an attempt to inspire confidence and followership. When you are ready to announce your plan, make it clear why you think this is important to the long-term health of the company. You can appeal to your investors' moral sensibilities, making a case that if your company expects the best from its people, the people should in return be able to expect the same from their company and that, as citizens of this world, those who run companies have a vested interest in making the world safer and more prosperous for everyone.

You can, if necessary, also appeal to more selfish interests. Professor Zeynep Ton, at MIT's Sloan School of Management, provides rich fodder through her research on how successful companies invest in employees. In her book, *The Good Jobs Strategy*, Ton examines how certain companies in traditionally low-skilled and low-paid industries have outperformed their competition by investing heavily in their employees, even when investors have criticized them for not keeping expenses down. In 2007, electronics retailer Circuit City fired 3,400 of its highest-paid workers in an attempt to cut costs and replaced them with lower-paid personnel. Meanwhile, Circuit City's largest competitor, Best Buy, invested heavily in its employees through high staffing levels and an increased focus on customer service. While Circuit City went out of business in 2009, Best

Buy continues to thrive, and its share price regularly exceeds investor expectations.

Ton also points to the relative performance of Sam's Club, which is owned by Walmart, versus its chief competitor, Costco. Pay at Costco is over 40 percent higher than that at Sam's Club, but employees return that money to the company through consistent high performance. Costco's sales are almost 70 percent higher than Sam's Club's, and a typical Costco employee outsells his typical Sam's Club counterpart by almost double. Costco's stock has also grown at a much faster rate over the past decade than Walmart's, proving that paying people more can actually be a boon for investors.[13]

Still, some investors will look at your move to pay a living wage as a forced sacrifice. To boost confidence, consider making your own sacrifice. Forgo any compensation based on equity or defer your vesting period to align with your long-term goals for the company. This will prove you are committed and are not trying to rob Peter to pay Paul.

Communicate Your Plan

The vast majority of Gravity employees did not know about the $70k plan until I announced it at an all-company meeting. While it was an amazing moment that I wouldn't change for the world,

---

13. Zeynep Ton, *The Good Jobs Strategy: How the Smartest Companies Invest in Employees to Lower Costs and Boost Profits* (New York: Houghton Mifflin Harcourt, 2014), 71.

I recommend you communicate your idea to your team long before you put an official plan in place because doing so will give you time to answer questions, alleviate concerns, and get feedback. How and when you do so is up to you, but I would advise announcing it as soon as you've made a commitment to putting a living wage in place and you've done enough research to know that your goal is feasible, even if it might take awhile to implement. You don't need to know exactly how you're going to raise wages or what sacrifices you're going to make to afford it, but you want to be confident that some positive change will happen in the not-too-distant future. If you don't, you run the risk of upsetting a lot of people on the off chance that the financials don't pencil out.

When you make the announcement, be sure to solicit feedback from people throughout your company. If your organization is large, consider arranging a town hall–style meeting or two in which people can share ideas, opinions, and concerns directly with executives and any other decision makers. You probably won't be able to please everyone, but if you listen to and consider their feedback, they will likely feel more comfortable with whatever final decision you make than they would if they had had no say at all.

Even if you're met with negative feedback, never back down from your commitment. People will criticize you. They will root for you to fail. They will call you naïve and question your fitness as a leader. Remember that their criticism comes from a place of fear—if you succeed, they'll be forced to rethink the way they see the world and how they do things. No one likes to be told they're wrong or have their perspective challenged, and that is exactly what you're trying to do.

What If You Really Can't Afford to Pay People More?

You've crunched the numbers and explored every possible option, and there is simply no way you can afford to pay your employees one dollar more without jeopardizing your business. If you are just starting out or run a small business on razor-thin margins, raising your employees' wages might not be possible for you right now. That doesn't mean you can't do anything to help your people thrive.

Are there other ways you can ease your employees' financial burden without increasing their pay? Could you let them work from home a few days a week, thus helping them save money on transportation? Could you change their schedules to overlap with school hours so they don't have to worry about childcare? Could you do what Stephan Aarstol at Tower Paddle Boards did and switch to a five-hour workday? If you're able, talk to your employees individually, or have your managers do so, and work with them to brainstorm ways to ease their financial burdens until you are in a position to increase their salaries.

Of course, the best way to get to that position is to grow your business so you can afford to pay a living wage. You can't do this alone, so why not turn to your people for help? One of the biggest mistakes companies make is treating their employees like expenses to be managed rather than human beings with their own innate creativity, intelligence, and capabilities. As a result, they fail to unlock the potential that these individuals have to offer, and the business suffers. This is especially true for traditionally low-wage jobs like those in retail or customer service. Because these roles don't require a lot of formal training or education and are known for their high turnover, many companies see the workers in these jobs as disposable. They don't invest time, energy, or money into developing them, even though research shows that companies that develop workers—including low-wage ones—are more successful over the long term than those that don't.[14]

No matter what industry you're in, how large your company is, or how much money you have in the bank, you can create good jobs for your employees by treating them with respect and dignity. Give them a sense of ownership in the business by empowering them to make decisions and offer suggestions that could improve the way you do things. Talk to them about their career goals and see if there's a way for you to help them develop skills that align with those goals. Create your own version of a "be your own CEO" culture so people feel they can have a direct impact on the success of your business. Create an environment where people enjoy coming to work and trust them with more responsibilities as their talents grow.

---

14. Ton, *The Good Jobs Strategy*, chapter 4.

Before long, you'll see the benefit of this investment reflected in the growth of your business, and you'll be able to share the rewards with the people who helped you earn them.

Investors

Unless you have a major stake in the companies you invest in, you probably have relatively little say in how much those companies pay their people. But you can still have an enormous influence over the decisions companies make, especially if you're investing in them directly. Companies want investors whose values align with their own, so choose to invest in those that value paying a living wage. When assessing a new opportunity, ask the company's leaders about their compensation philosophies and how they develop their employees. Do they offer benefits, parental leave, and paid time off? How much do they train employees, and does that training continue throughout their tenure at the organization? How often do they promote from within? What is their annual turnover rate? These indicators can help you assess how likely they are to support a living wage, even if that's not their current policy. Evaluating a company based on these metrics will also help you make better long-term investments, since companies that take care of their workers tend to be more sustainable than those that don't.

Don't be shy about your stance on employee pay. Share it on your website. Talk about it on social media. Write articles about it on LinkedIn or other platforms that business leaders read.

Become an outspoken advocate for the living wage, so much so that people associate you with that cause. Doing so will not only help spread the word about the importance of pay equity, it will also attract like-minded companies to you and bring you more opportunities to have an impact.

Most importantly, rethink your purpose as an investor. When most people talk about investing, they discuss how to make the most money in the shortest amount of time and typically end the conversation there. But at what point does more money become worthless? At what point does another dollar in your pocket stop improving your well-being? At what point will you be satisfied? At what point will you have enough?

What would happen if you decided the purpose of investing was not to make money but to help worthy businesses thrive? We've come to believe that money is an end unto itself and have adopted it as the standard yardstick for success. But what if we looked at money for what it is—a tool to help us exchange goods and services that we want and need. What if you started using your money and power as an investor to support companies that pay a living wage and are committed to helping their communities thrive?

Your job as an investor is to make money, but that doesn't have to be your purpose. Take the time to figure out what you want your life's purpose to be and commit to letting that purpose guide you through your decisions. If you're afraid of the effect this might have on your career, take comfort in the words of John Bogle, founder of the Vanguard Group, inventor of the index fund, and one of history's most successful and

innovative investors: "Success cannot be measured solely—
or even primarily—in monetary terms, nor in terms of the
amount of power one may exercise over others, nor in the
illusory fame of inevitably transitory public notice," he wrote in
his book *Enough*. "But it *can* be measured in our contributions
to building a better world, in helping our fellow man, and in
raising children who themselves become loving human beings
and good citizens. Success, in short, can be measured not in
what we attain for ourselves, but in what we contribute to our
society."

Government and Policy Makers

I am not a politician, but I can't discuss solutions to our income
inequality problem without discussing the role our government
can play in addressing it. There is not enough room here for me
to make detailed comments or policy recommendations, but
because I am a business owner, and politicians often cite the
effect of wage policies on businesses, I feel it is my duty to share
at least a broad perspective.

The primary reason government has been slow to address
income inequality is not because those in power lack the ability
to do so but because they lack the will. While politicians like
Senator Bernie Sanders, Representative Alexandria Ocasio-
Cortez, and several others on the Left have made income
inequality a primary focus of their agendas, there are still many
politicians who believe businesses should be allowed to set their

own wages and that mandating a higher minimum wage—let alone a living wage—will destroy our economy and turn us into a socialist backwater the likes of Venezuela. They believe this despite the fact that the United States—the world's largest economy—has some of the worst inequality among developed nations.[15]

What's more, even though we like to think of ourselves as the greatest country on earth, we are consistently ranked as less happy than more socialist countries like Finland, Denmark, New Zealand, and Canada.[16] The Declaration of Independence asserts that government exists to protect its citizens' "unalienable Rights," among which are "Life, Liberty, and the pursuit of Happiness." Somewhere along the way, we came to believe this meant the government's purpose is to protect a few people's ability to amass astounding wealth while others can't afford life's necessities. People defend the unbridled power of the largest corporations by citing "freedom." For them, "freedom" means freedom from government, not the freedom to live a peaceful, dignified existence without fear of persecution, rejection, or violence. Instead of viewing government as the founders intended it—as a force designed to balance the interests of all citizens in

order to create a prosperous and peaceful society—they view it as an obstacle to amassing the most wealth possible. We, as a nation,

---

15. OECD Data, "Income Inequality," accessed October 29, 2019, https://doi.org/10.1787/459aa7f1-en.

16. World Happiness Report, "Finland Again Is the Happiest Country in the World," March 20, 2019, https://worldhappiness.report/news/finland-again-is-the-happiest-country-in-the-world/.

have misplaced our priorities. Fortunately, our political system endows those we elect to office with the power to create change.

If you're reading this, I assume you're someone who wants to help create this change and I don't need to convince you why guaranteeing people a living wage is important. While I'm not a policy expert, I feel strongly that there are a few things government can and must do to help reduce inequality in America by supporting a living wage for all.

Create a Market that Promotes a Living Wage

Staunch market capitalists argue that any attempt by government to set wages will interfere with the market in a way that will have devastating effects on the economy. Citing Adam Smith's "invisible hand," they believe businesses should only be required to pay employees what the market deems they are worth. But this line of thinking fails to acknowledge that markets do not exist in a vacuum. They are shaped by the laws and norms that govern a society. For the past forty or so years, our laws have favored employers rather than employees. Government has removed regulations, imposed limits on unions, lowered corporate tax rates, succumbed to lobbying efforts, and encouraged consolidation, all of which have helped drive labor costs down. As former secretary of labor Robert Reich sums it up in his book *Saving Capitalism*, "The meritocratic claim that people are paid what they are worth in the market is a tautology that begs the questions of how the market is organized and whether that organization is morally and economically defensible. In truth, income and wealth increasingly depend on who has the power to set the rules of the game."

If we want to create a society that supports all workers instead of just a powerful few, our public servants must accept their responsibility to make a fairer market. One way to do this would be to raise the federal minimum wage, which is currently set at $7.25 an hour and has not been raised since 2009. The federal wage need not be $15 an hour, as is the case in some states, since the cost of living varies widely from region to region. But putting the onus on state and local governments to set their own minimums pits them against one another in a race to the bottom as they compete to attract large corporations to their areas with the promises of low labor costs.

Another option is to provide a tax incentive to companies that pay a living wage and/or those that don't pay executives beyond a certain percentage more than their lowest-paid workers. This would still give businesses the freedom to make their own decisions but would encourage higher pay and help to increase wages across the board.

In its role as an employer, government can also increase wages to create a better market for workers. Not only does this mean paying all government workers a living wage for their locale, it also requires raising salaries of traditionally underpaid professionals, like public-school teachers, to better reflect their value to society. A free public education is something we have come to take for granted, to the point where we've devalued the role of having high-quality teachers educate our children, especially those who are most vulnerable. If we want to set teachers up to be successful, we need to pay them enough to live a productive and fulfilling life. And if we want to attract the best people to a career in education, we need to create a career path that is seen as desirable and dignified.

Another way to even the playing field is to promote entrepreneurship and small businesses. Forty-eight percent of all money spent at local businesses is cycled back into local communities. By contrast, just 14 percent of dollars spent at national chains stays in town.[17] Small businesses create more jobs than large ones and bring vitality to their communities. When politicians talk about helping businesses, they should distinguish between small and large businesses and design policies that encourage entrepreneurship while ensuring that successful, established businesses pay their fair share in the form of wages, benefits, and taxes.

By holding businesses accountable for taking care of their employees and communities, we will ultimately create a better market that serves all of us instead of just those who are powerful and wealthy enough to set the rules in their favor. In turn we will revitalize the middle class, ensure upward mobility for the most disadvantaged Americans, and reduce dependency

---

17. American Independent Business Alliance, "The Multiplier Effect of Local Independent Businesses," accessed October 29, 2019, https://www.amiba. net/ resources/multiplier-effect/.

on social safety net programs like welfare. When we remember our original values of protecting life, liberty, and the pursuit of happiness, we will become a much stronger, more unified, more prosperous America for all.

There is a lot of work to be done before every American will be guaranteed a living wage. In the face of so much inequality, uncertainty, and divisiveness, you probably feel overwhelmed by all of these suggestions. At the end of the day, however, you don't need to follow any of my advice in order to make a difference. All you have to do is ask yourself one question: What am I willing to sacrifice in order to make a difference and do what I think is right? If you believe that everyone deserves a living wage, consider what you would give up in order to see that happen. Are you willing to give up wealth? Status? Reputation? Relationships? Safety? What would you be able to accomplish tomorrow if you made that sacrifice today?

It's not an easy question, and it requires an immense amount of courage to put something you care about so deeply and worked so hard to get on the line when you don't know the outcome. But this is what leadership is all about: going against what is safe or what is certain or what is easy in order to accomplish something truly great.

I have faith in you.

Appendix 2

Facts and Figures to Help You Fight
Income Inequality

IF YOU TAKE NOTHING else away from this book, I hope you better understand the critical point income inequality has reached in our country. If we continue on this trajectory, it's not unrealistic to expect that we'll soon be living in a plutocracy— even if we continue to call ourselves a democracy. When I first announced our $70k policy in 2015, I hoped Gravity would be successful so that we could prove to the world that there was a better way of doing business. I trusted that, in turn, more people would prioritize paying a living wage and reducing inequality, but things have only gotten worse. I now realize it's going to take a lot more than one company to right the wrongs in our economy, which is why I'm counting on you to help me in this fight.

Throughout this book, I have pointed to various income

inequality statistics as well as findings from Gravity and other sources that show what happens when companies pay a living wage. I often quote these statistics when making my case to others, and I hope you will, too. To make it easier, I have listed some of the most compelling research in the pages that follow. If you find other research or want to share your perspectives with me directly, you can find me on social media @danpriceseattle.

Income Inequality Stats

- According to the Census Bureau, income inequality in the United States is the highest it's been in fifty years, despite a strong economy and an overall increase in median household income.[18]

- In 2017, 82 percent of all new wealth created worldwide went to the richest 1 percent of individuals.[19]

- Since 1995, the median net worth of the top 1 percent of Americans has grown by 187 percent. In the same time period, the median net worth of the American middle class has grown by just 7 percent.

---

18. Telford, September 26, 2019.

19. Oxfam, January 28, 2018.

- Before 2010, the American middle class owned more wealth than the top 1 percent. Today, the top 1 percent owns 29 percent of American wealth, compared to just 18 percent for the entire middle class.[20]

- Average pre-tax income for the bottom half of Americans has grown by just 3 percent since 1980, even though overall incomes have grown by 65 percent. In Europe, average pre-tax income for the bottom half of the population has grown by 40 percent in the same time frame, while overall incomes have grown by 51 percent.[21]

- The top .01 percent of Americans earn 875 times more annually than the poorest half of Americans, up from 188 times more in 1970.[22]

---

20. Isabel V. Sawhill and Christopher Pulliam, "Six facts about wealth in the United States," Brookings, June 25, 2019, https://www.brookings.edu/blog/up-front/2019/06/25/six-facts-about-wealth-in-the-united-states/.

21. Thomas Blanchet, Lucas Chancel, and Amory Gethin, "Why US inequality is higher than Europe's," Zawya, November 13, 2019, https://www.zawya.com/mena/en/economy/story/Why_US_inequality_is_higher_than_Europes-ZAWYA20191113031701/.

22. Sam Pizzigati, "Are America's Rich Getting Tired of Winning Yet?" Inequality.org, December 12, 2019, https://inequality.org/great-divide/are-the-rich-getting-tired-of-winning-yet/.

CEO Pay

- CEOs at America's 350 largest companies earn an average of 321 times more than their median workers. In 1965, that ratio was 20:1.[23]

- Although net worker productivity increased by 69.6 percent between 1979 and 2018, net hourly compensation (adjusted for inflation) increased by only 11.6 percent. By contrast, CEO compensation rose 979 percent over roughly the same time period, despite the fact that the stock market (a key indicator of company performance) grew by only 637 percent.[24]

- Companies who pay their CEOs below the median salary for their sector outperform those who pay their CEOs more than the median.[25]

----

23. Lawrence Mishel and Jessica Schieder, "CEO compensation surged in 2017," Economic Policy Institute, August 16, 2018, https://www.epi.org/publication/ceo-compensation-surged-in-2017/.

24. Economic Policy Institute, "The Productivity-Pay Gap," https://www.epi.org/productivity-pay-gap/.

25. Ric Marshall, "Are CEOs Paid for Performance?" MSCI, July 25, 2016, https://www.msci.com/www/blog-posts/are-ceos-paid-for-performance-/0410455074.

Cost of Living

- The federal minimum wage is $7.25 an hour. It has not been raised since 2009. A full-time minimum-wage worker earns $15,080 a year, which is below the poverty line for a family of two in America. Adjusted for inflation, the federal minimum wage is worth 25 percent less than it was in 1968.[26]

- Since the 1990s, the cost of childcare in the United States has grown at twice the rate of inflation.[27]

- Between 2008 and 2018, the cost of attending college increased by more than 25 percent. Since 1978, the cost has more than doubled when adjusted for inflation.[28]

- Adjusted for inflation, it costs almost twice as much (1.78 times) to buy a new home in America today

---

26. TopCHRO, "Minimum Wages Are Causing Maximum Discomfort. Hustle Up Reality Check!," February 22, 2019, https://www.topchro.com/article/minimum-wages-are-causing-maximum-discomfort-hustle-up-reality-check.

27. Danielle Kurtzleben, "5 charts that show child care in the US is broken," Vox, July 17, 2014, https://www.vox.com/2014/7/17/5909651/5-charts-that-show-child-care-in-the-us-is-broken.

28. Abigail Hess, "The cost of college increased by more than 25% in the last 10 years—here's why," CNBC.com, December 13, 2019, https://www.cnbc.com/2019/12/13/cost-of-college-increased-by-more-than-25percent-in-the-last-10-years.html.

than it did fifty years ago.[29]

- Adjusted for inflation, the average American household spends twice as much per year on health care as they did in 1980.[30]

- In 2000, when unemployment was at 4 percent, 6 percent of Americans were on food stamps. In 2019, with unemployment at 3.6 percent (the lowest in fifty years), nearly 11 percent of Americans were on food stamps.[31]

- Only 40 percent of Americans say they would be able to cover a $1,000 emergency expense (such as a car repair or emergency-room visit) from savings.[32]

---

29.   United States Census Bureau, "Median and Average Sales Prices of New Homes Sold in the United States," https://www.census.gov/construction/nrs/pdf/uspricemon.pdf.

30.   Megan Leonhardt, "Americans now spend twice as much on health care as they did in the 1980s," CNBC.com, October 9, 2019, https://www.cnbc.com/2019/10/09/americans-spend-twice-as-much-on-health-care-today-as-in-the-1980s.html.

31.   Laura Reiley, "Trump administration tightens work requirements for SNAP, which could cut hundreds of thousands from food stamps," *Washington Post*, December 4, 2019, https://www.washingtonpost.com/business/2019/12/04/trump-administration-tightens-work-requirements-snap-which-could-cut-hundreds-thousands-food-stamps/.

32.   Adrian D. Garcia, "Survey: Most Americans wouldn't cover a $1k emergency with savings," Bankrate, January 16, 2019, https://www.bankrate.com/banking/savings/financial-security-january-2019/.

Benefits of Paying a Living Wage

- Research consistently shows that companies that pay higher wages to typically low-wage workers are rewarded with increased productivity, lower employee turnover, improved customer service, and, ultimately, higher profits.[33]

- Workers who earn a living wage are happier and less depressed than those who don't.[34] Happier workers are more productive.[35]

- Research consistently shows that the benefits associated with raising wages (e.g., improvement to workers' well-being, increased productivity, lower turnover, greater efficiency) typically outweigh the costs (e.g., increased costs to consumers, job losses, lower profits). In many cases, actual costs end up being much lower than estimates

---

33. Justin Wolfers and Jan Zilinsky, "Higher Wages for Low-Income Workers Lead to Higher Productivity," Peterson Institute for International Economics, January 13, 2015, https://www.piie.com/blogs/realtime-economic-issues-watch/higher-wages-low-income-workers-lead-higher-productivity. See also Ton, *The Good Jobs Strategy*.

34. Kirsten Weir, "A living wage," *Monitor on Psychology* 47, no. 4 (April 2016): 28, https://www.apa.org/monitor/2016/04/living-wage.

35. Clément S. Bellet, Jan-Emmanuel De Neve, and George Ward, "Does Employee Happiness Have an Impact on Productivity?" *Saïd Business School WP* 2019–13, October 14, 2019, https://papers.ssrn.com/sol3/papers.cfm?abstract_id=3470734&download=yes.

and are offset by higher productivity and efficiency.[36]

Impact of the $70k Minimum Wage at Gravity Payments

The $70k minimum wage was announced in April 2015. Since that time, we have witnessed several positive trends in both our business and the lives of our employees.

Human Impact

- Before the $70k announcement, Gravity employees had an average of 0–2 babies per year. After $70k, an average of 7–8 new babies have been born per year. This is an increase of roughly 400 percent per year despite the headcount growing by just 75 percent in that five-year period.

- Since the $70k announcement, at least twenty team members (more than 10 percent of the company)

---

36. Jeff Thompson and Jeff Chapman, "The economic impact of local living wages," Economic Policy Institute, February 15, 2006, https://www.epi.org/publication/bp170/; Michael Reich, Sylvia A. Allegretto, and Claire Montialoux, "The Employment Effects of a $15 Minimum Wage in the U.S. and in Mississippi: A Simulation Approach," Institute for Research on Labor and Employment, March 1, 2019, https://irle.berkeley.edu/the-employment-effects-of-a-15-minimum-wage-in-the-u-s-and-in-mississippi/; and Allana Akhtar, "The $15 minimum wage was supposed [to] end in a restaurant apocalypse. Here's how 5 major cities proved the prophets of doom wrong," Business Insider, August 16, 2019, https://www.businessinsider.com/restaurant-industries-impacted-by-wage-increases-in-5-cities-2019-8.

have purchased a house for the first time.

- Personal individual 401(k) contributions have more than doubled since the announcement (155 percent increase).

- More than 70 percent of those at the company with debt have been able to pay it down, with over one-third of them paying off over 50 percent of their total debt.

Business Impact

- Dollars processed (a key metric used to measure growth in the payments industry) has almost tripled from $3.8 billion in 2014 to $11.2 billion in 2019.

- Our customer base has nearly doubled since 2014.

- Employee headcount has increased by 70 percent since 2015.

- Customer attrition has maintained at 25+ percent below the industry average.

- Annual employee turnover has dropped from pre-$70k levels of 40–60 percent to 15–30 percent.

- According to Gravity's 2019 annual employee survey, 76 percent of employees report being engaged at work, compared to just 34 percent of workers worldwide.[37]

- Average tenure of employees is over a year longer than that of Square, one of our most well-known competitors, (3.3 versus 2.3 years).

Impact on Equality

- The highest-paid executive at Gravity earns just four times more than the lowest-paid employee at the company.

- There is no gender wage gap at Gravity.

Further Reading

The following books delve deep into the topics of income inequality, economic and workplace trends, employee motivation, executive and worker compensation, the cost of living, discrimination, the history of capitalism, and other topics that have helped inform my understanding of compensation and employee well-being. They are all excellent and worth your time.

---

37. Jim Harter, "Employee Engagement on the Rise in the U.S.," Gallup, August 26, 2018, https://news.gallup.com/poll/241649/employee-engagement-rise.aspx.

Can American Capitalism Survive?: Why Greed Is Not Good, Opportunity Is Not Equal, and Fairness Won't Make Us Poor by Steven Pearlstein.

Dark Money: The Hidden History of the Billionaires Behind the Rise of the Radical Right by Jane Mayer.

Drive: The Surprising Truth about What Motivates Us by Daniel H. Pink.

The End of Loyalty: The Rise and Fall of Good Jobs in America by Rick Wartzman.

The Good Jobs Strategy: How the Smartest Companies Invest in Employees to Lower Costs and Boost Profits by Zeynep Ton.

On the Clock: What Low-Wage Work Did to Me and How It Drives America Insane by Emily Guendelsberger.

Saving Capitalism: For the Many, Not the Few by Robert B. Reich.

The Vanishing Middle Class: Prejudice and Power in a Dual Economy by Peter Temin.

Winners Take All: The Elite Charade of Changing the World by Anand Giridharadas.

Index

About the Author

DAN PRICE founded Gravity Payments when he was just nineteen years old. His mission was—and is—to help hardworking small-business owners compete against larger corporations by making credit card processing transparent, fair, and easy. Today, nearly twenty thousand independent businesses across all fifty states trust Gravity as their processor.

In 2015, Dan captured national attention when he decided to slash his salary by more than 90 percent and raise the company's minimum salary to $70,000 a year. Since then, he has become an outspoken advocate for income equality and, through speeches, articles, and media appearances, has consistently encouraged other business owners to take responsibility for the well-being of their employees. His leadership has earned him many awards, most notably *Entrepreneur* magazine's Entrepreneur of 2014 and the Small Business Administration's 2010 National Young Entrepreneur of the Year, awarded to him by President Barack Obama. He lives in Seattle with his rescue dog, Mikey.

CPSIA information can be obtained
at www.ICGtesting.com
Printed in the USA
LVHW032234260221
680081LV00016B/77/J